THE GIRL GUIDE

by Marawa Ibrahim

Illustrated by Sinem Erkas

# 50 LESSONS
## in learning to ♥ your changing body

How to read this book:
dip in, dip out, start at the back, skip to the front or read it straight through but turn to it in times of need!

Hi, I'm Marawa!

This is me at ten

This is me, now

Hello! I hope this book finds you well, snuggled up in a comfy spot with a hot chocolate, or on a bus heading home... however you got here – HI! This book has been a dream project for me since I was ten, because around that time my body started doing all these weird new things and I had so many questions and not enough answers. Twenty years on I feel like I have some of it figured out, so I wanted to put it all together and share it with you. This book is made to dip in and out of, and includes a whole bunch of my own embarrassing stories!

I spent my teenage years in Melbourne, Australia, and when I was young, my mum encouraged me to do a lot of sport, which I LOVED and finally led me into doing a Circus Arts degree at university! Since then, I've spent my life travelling around as an international show-girl, and now I work with young women just like yourself through my hula-hooping troupe, The Majorettes.

But don't get me wrong, it's not all glamour. I still get my period at awkward moments and, occasionally, have to deal with unsinkable poos. Sometimes, something happens that is so weird you would think it is A) too embarrassing to ever mention or B) surely the only time it's ever happened in the history of womankind – but we have all been there! And despite this I am still 100% convinced that being a girl is the BEST! Our bodies are AMAZING – and are capable of doing lots of great things. It's a great time to be female – you only need to do a little research to know that womankind has had a pretty rough run through history – but now we are crusading into the 21st century, breaking down stereotypes everywhere. You can do ANYTHING you want with your life! Go to the Moon! Start an organic toothbrush company! Have a million babies! Hormones may be annoying till you work them out but once you do, life can be just as fun as ever. KNOWLEDGE IS POWER. Get to know how your body works and how to make it work for you.

Go forth, little sister,
Marawa xx

# 1

# ALL EYES ON YOU

• • • • •

When you start looking like a little lady, people might start TREATING you like a woman. Boys and men might begin looking at you a little differently, which can be nice or not-so-nice (see the 'That Was Weird' chapter). But everyone – friends, mums, the lady in the shop – might start talking to you differently, too. This can be uncomfortable, especially if they say something about your body and you are just getting used to your new shape yourself. You don't want someone pointing out that you have boobs or have put on weight. I remember my friend's mum coming over to our house and announcing in front of EVERYONE that I had put on 'so much weight – gosh' and I was looking 'so round'! My friend was even more embarrassed than me, I think – I just thought it was kind of annoying. I mean, I wasn't trying to make my body look different, it was doing it on its own!

Clothes
that used to fit were
suddenly really tight, or
too short. Sometimes it
was fun and I was excited about being
bigger and stronger and other times I wanted it
to stop so I could just stay where I was forever.

It was a weird feeling, too, realising that the 'invisible kid' label was starting to dissolve. I had younger brothers and sisters so I was always desperate to be included with the adults – not the kids. But when things began to change and I was no longer lumped in with the kids ('oh the kids are outside'; 'the kids are watching TV'), suddenly adults were asking me questions and wanting my opinions and thoughts on things. In some ways this was great and made me feel grown-up, but I was also confused about what the right thing to say was. I suddenly felt a bit daunted. I wanted to give the right answer to every question – the smart answer. But often I would feel uncomfortable and in the spotlight, or find myself going along with conversations that I don't think I fully understood.

So it can be really frustrating and annoying. Sometimes you feel like you're being treated like a child and then, when people start treating you like an adult, the responsibility that comes with it can seem unfair! My advice? Don't feel in a rush to join the adult table! You can take your time – it's nice to be able to float between adult-land and kids-ville for a while. ☺

# 2

# BOOBS, BREASTS, BAZOOKAS

· · · · · ·

Boobs are great! Once you get used to them...

Some grow bit-by-bit; some seem to appear overnight. Big or small, they are not going away, so embrace your breasts and look after them.

My friend's really hurt when they were growing and felt hot and itchy – she was always afraid of people knocking into her chest and went around with her arms crossed over them.

Mine appeared like balloons – one minute I was flat, the next they were there! Or that's how it felt. I liked them, but suddenly running, jumping and all the things I loved doing became a lot harder. I hated that! I wanted to be able to jump up and down without this extra weight literally dragging me down.

Mum bought me the ugliest sports bra I had ever seen. I hated the look of it so much but it did hold me in place and allow me to run

My first ugly
sports bra

the way I wanted to, so I wore it. BUT I put my cuter, less supportive sports bras over the top and prayed that no one would see the monster straps of the nuclear warheads holding

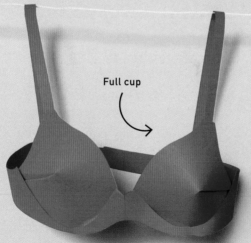

Full cup

my boobs in place. These days I wear different bras for different occasions, but while your
boobs are growing, it's best (and most comfortable) to get non-wired bras without too

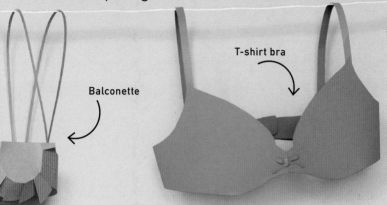

T-shirt bra

Balconette

many fiddly bits. Also, different shapes suit
different shapes! Try on a LOT before you buy
– one size does NOT fit all.

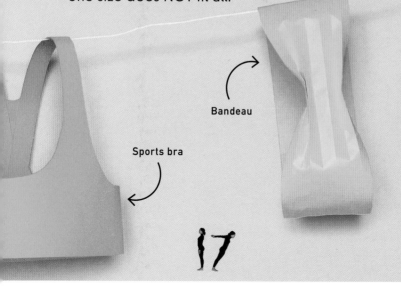

Bandeau

Sports bra

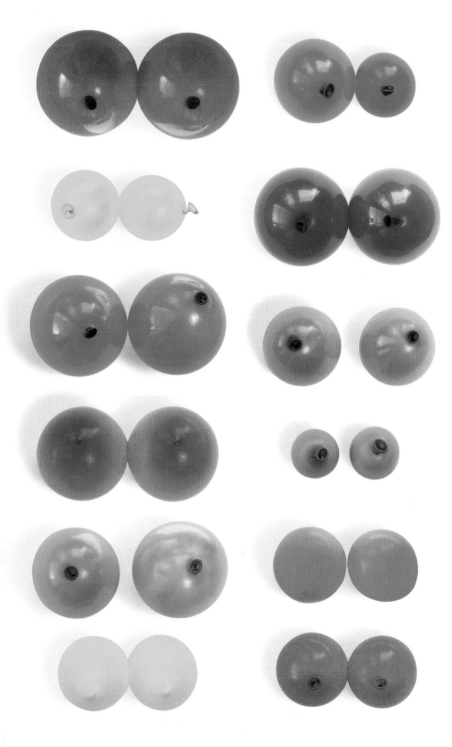

I had a friend in secondary school whose bra straps were always falling down her shoulder; she didn't realise that you could actually tighten them! Most importantly, get your bra FITTED. The bra-fitting lady at the shop sees boobs ALL DAY, so just remember your new boobs are only new to you, not her.

Guessing your own size can mean that you put up with loads of discomfort – straps that are too tight, clasps digging into you and scratchy lace – ugghh... My boobs changed size every year, so it's worth getting fitted regularly, especially when you're still growing. Also, it is COMPLETELY NORMAL to have:

One boob much bigger than the other

Hair, freckles and moles

Stretch marks

Boobs pointing in different directions

Big, sticky-outy nipples

Tiny nipples that only pop out when you're cold

Oh and... loads of other stuff. If you're unsure about ANYTHING, you can always ask your doctor.

Blue veins

# 3

# DOT-to-DOT

· · · · ·

Changes to your body's hormones often produce... SPOTS! I managed to get through my teenage years with barely any, but my skin recently started really breaking out! Spots can break out on your face, your chest, your back and even your bum! DON'T TOUCH 'EM – it's just gonna make 'em worse. The best thing is to keep them oil-free. Try using a very gentle cleanser (not soap) to wipe away oil, sweat and dirt from air pollution. I use dots of a clay face mask on spots overnight to dry them out, and clear witch-hazel ointment during the day (which is antiseptic, too). If your spots are really painful or won't go away, you may have acne. It's annoying, but it can be treated and you don't have to suffer. Get an adult to make an appointment for you with your doctor.

Don't panic! You might despair, but don't let spots ruin your week. Take a deep breath and remember this is temporary.

Spots hurt! Ice or a cold flannel will soothe them. If a spot explodes, get some antiseptic on there so it doesn't get infected.

Cleanse! If you're having a break-out, cleanse your skin twice a day. Remember: don't use regular soap – it's too harsh.

Drink loads! Water's so good for your body. It flushes out all the toxins and is great for your skin – keep glugging!

Avoid sugar! Cutting down on soft drinks and sugary snacks is healthier all-round and should really help your skin.

No squeezing! It's so tempting, I know, but I promise this will just make them worse. Keep them clean, dry and try not to touch!

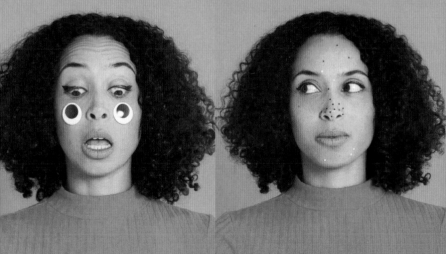

Stand back! Spots always feel waaay bigger than they are. Stand away from the mirror to look at them. See? Much better!

Blackheads are your skin's 'breathing holes' blocked with dirt. Taking care of your skin is the best way to avoid them.

# 4

# BRACE FACE

· · · · · ·

I had braces. If you don't have them, you probably know someone who does. I didn't want them; I was CONVINCED that I would kiss someone and we would get stuck together and have to go to hospital and someone would take our picture and we would end up in the paper as 'The World's Stupidest Teenagers'. (I hadn't actually kissed anyone by this stage.)

Braces can be painful. After all, rearranging the teeth in your face is no small feat! BUT, if you are lucky enough to get them, be grateful. Straight teeth are a luxury and are with you for life. At the time, being a 'brace face' felt like a LIFE sentence, but now it feels like it was barely a moment. Though now, every time I bite into an apple, I am so happy I won't have to spend an hour picking it out of my teeth.

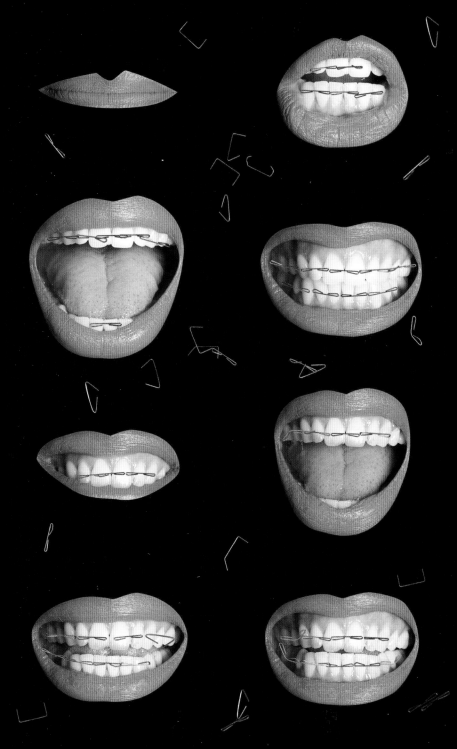

# 5

# SWEAT... LIKE A GIRL!

· · · · · ·

Newsflash: men, women, girls and boys sweat. There's no way around it – just like all human beings, YOU'VE GOTTA SWEAT! Whether it's from exercise, excitement, heat or anger, your body sweats to help cool you down. But sometimes with sweat comes a smell – and often we want to try and disguise it. I remember telling my mum that I needed deodorant – I smelled like sweat and I didn't want to. I was sure everyone on the train could smell me. What I didn't realise was that your body's natural smell is actually often pleasant to other people, even if it's strong, so long as it is FRESH! But I thought I should smell like an air freshener: I wanted the smell of roses to come out of me. So, I got a deodorant. But there are things I wish I'd known about it...

Nearly all deodorant has aluminium in it – you can see it listed in the ingredients. Aluminium blocks sweat from coming out of your armpits.

This is:

### GOOD

because the sweat stops, so you stay dry under your arms. Plus, if you don't like the smell of your sweat, it will be masked by the scent of your deodorant.

### BAD

because sweat is your body's natural way of cooling itself down. Doctors advise that aluminium is not meant to be rubbed all over your skin! You can get natural deodorants that don't have aluminium – BUT – they are less effective at covering the smell of sweat.

So it's a tricky one. But there are other things that you can do...

Like I said, the smell of sweat isn't actually unpleasant when it's fresh. Sometimes I really like it! But to keep fresh, here are some tips...

### Showers

It sounds obvious, but just make sure you wash really well every day, with soap! Get in under your armpits and scrub!

### Natural deodorant

BEFORE you get sweaty, use a natural deodorant on your clean skin. You can 'top up' during the day if you really feel like you need to – I sometimes do if I play sport and get sweaty – but it's your call. Some people love the smell of their own sweat. BREATHE DEEP!

### Clothes

This one is really important. Natural fibres, like cotton or wool, allow your skin to breathe. Synthetic fabrics, like polyester or acrylic, don't. They just lock the heat in like plastic wrap. It makes a HUGE difference to the sweat situation, so always read the label.

# 6

# YOU ARE NOT ALONE

· · · · ·

… even though sometimes it really, REALLY feels like you are. I used to have two types of 'feeling alone'. One was when there was a party and EVERYONE in the world was going and my dad would not let me go (this was a theme for most of my secondary school years). I would be so mad and feel like the whole world was turning but no one knew or cared that I existed. Sitting at home, bored, in my room with nothing to do… ugghh. It was the worst.

The other type of 'alone' would just come out of nowhere: all of a sudden, I would feel like nothing made sense and that the world was a huge place – lost in a giant universe. I knew deep down that I had friends and people loved me but in that moment, right then, I just felt really alone – like nobody understood what I was feeling or thinking about, and nobody REALLY cared

about me. I could usually snap out of this by talking myself back to logic-land, or calling a friend or writing in a journal. Sometimes you've just got to get all those thoughts out and then everything feels normal again.

There are loads of other emotions that kicked in when I was at secondary school. Feeling awkward – so awkward that even just saying 'hello' to someone seemed like an obstacle course I was sure to fail. Was it 'hi', 'hey', 'wassaaaaap', a hug, high-five or a wave? And then I'd end up making some weird squeaking sound that was DEFINITELY not cool. Feeling embarrassed, especially in public, was THE WORST. Although I can't even remember what I was embarrassed about (which shows how pointless it was), I do remember spending days agonising over embarrasing moments, and playing them over and over in my mind.

I wish I could have NOT stressed about these things and just moved on, but maybe that's all part of the process. These days, I embarrass myself regularly but I don't let it bother me... I guess I just needed more practice.

# 7

# WITNESS THE FITNESS

· · · · ·

Being active is essential to a healthy lifestyle. But getting motivated to move can be almost harder than the exercise itself! Overcoming self-consciousness is also a huge hurdle. I remember when I started getting heavier I would think and think about starting to exercise but never quite get around to doing it... I always had a good excuse! I think I also wanted to be perfect at everything – or at least good at it – so learning a new sport or anything that made me feel vulner-able, or potentially laughed-at, just had a huge 'DON'T GO THERE' sticker on it.

But if you are going to look after your body, you have to get that heart rate UP, UP, UP, and you need to sweat. Not only is exercise great for you long-term, but short-term you get a rush of endor-phins, which are the feel-good chemicals that are released into your brain, making you feel happy

and good about yourself. What's not to like? The only question is: which kind of exercise to pick? Personally I find so many types of exercise B-O-R-I-N-G. It's so important to find something that you actually enjoy! OBVIOUSLY I am biased but I think hula-hooping is the most fun exercise ever. And also roller-skating, skipping and dancing like I am on 'Soul Train'. But there are loads of other things out there – you just need to find your groove. If you find starting to exercise a real chore, you can work it into your week by setting a goal to do 20 minutes, three times a week. It's easy to find time if you plan ahead – 20 minutes first thing in the morning is a great way to start the day and get you moving! If you need a little head start, you can also exercise in private before unleashing your new skills on the world! But try not to feel too self-conscious. Everyone knows that you have to start at the start – even champions were beginners once. Sport is a great way to build confidence. The hardest part is just getting started!

# 8

# CLIP CLOP — NOT HOT

· · · · ·

I think I was 17 when I got my first pair of heels. I loved the look and idea of them but did NOT like the pain in the balls of my feet after wearing them. Heels also stop you moving freely – so at your age, there's no WAY would I wear them! Your bones 'n' joints are still growing and wearing heels can throw everything in your whole body out of alignment. Heels are terrible for your posture and back. Even if you feel your mind is fully formed, your bones are not! On average, girls' bones strop growing between 14 and 15 – this is when bones stop being bendy and have a lower risk of being thrown out of joint. So at the very least, wait till then. And even then, remember: heels are great for a couple of hours at a time but not during the day, when you're running around doing stuff. If I go out in heels, I always make sure I have a pair of flats with me too.

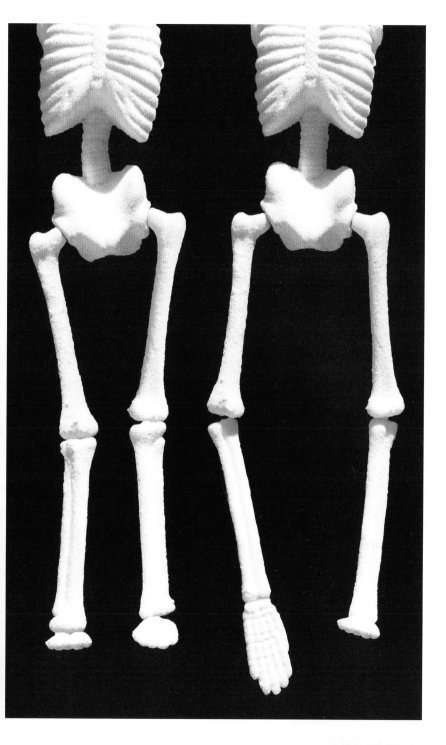

# THE PEE STORY

· · · · ·

When I was 14, I wet my pants. It was a normal day. I walked home – in my sports uniform – and as per usual, as soon as I saw the house I needed to pee. This still happens to me now – when I get home I immediately need to pee. Anyway, on this particular day I didn't have a key, which was fine because there was a spare around the back. Except that there wasn't. So far, no problem – I knew how to climb in through the upstairs bedroom window. So I

44

climbed onto the roof. And for the first time in the history of my house, all the windows were locked. Now I was getting annoyed. This was before mobile phones, so I couldn't call to see who was coming home or was nearby and I was too embarrassed to ask the neighbours. I sat in the back garden trying to come up with a plan. I really, REALLY needed to pee. I lay on my back, thinking that might help. Then I propped my legs up against the wall. That made it worse. I started getting shooting pains. I thought about sit-ups and how strong my stomach was and how I should be able to hold it in. I thought about squatting down somewhere and just peeing, but then I kept thinking someone would hear me and look over the fence, and see my vagina and I would DIE of embarrassment.

So I squeezed and squeezed, cursing every single one of my family members for not leaving a window open or a key out. Then... I felt a little trickle start. Oh my God, this was happening. I went and stood under the clothes line and silently wet my pants. And my tracksuit bottoms. And my socks. And my shoes – which I kicked off almost in time. It was warm and unstoppable – it must have been a whole litre. I was mortified. And then cold. I took a pair of my mum's pyjama bottoms off the washing line and then silently and awkwardly peeled out of my wet tracksuit trousers and into her pyjamas – which stuck to my legs as I hadn't dried them. Oh my God, the horror. Literally as I was putting them on, I heard my mum's car pull in to the drive. I STORMED out to inform her that she was the worst mother ever for not leaving me a key, but when I got out front she was talking to a girl from my school, who was walking past. They both looked at me, standing there in pyjama trousers and half a school uniform. I said, 'Oh, hi,' and then helped her unpack the car, like everything was fine. Worst day ever.

46

# VAGINA

• • • • •

So, when you learn about your vagina, you find out that you have a hole going up inside you, behind your pee hole, that you can stick your finger right up! I thought that was SO WEIRD! Where was the end? Was there an end? What else was up there? What about when I go swimming? Does the water go up there – DOES IT COME BACK OUT? AM I DRINKING THAT WATER?! (The answers are: your cervix; yes; your womb, fallopian tubes and other stuff; what about it?; probably; probably; probably!) I don't think I sat and actually LOOKED at my vagina till I was about 14 because it kind of grossed me out – there was hair and a new smell and all sorts. Was this the unique, special thing everyone made it out to be?

50

SAY IT LOUD AND SAY IT PROUD:

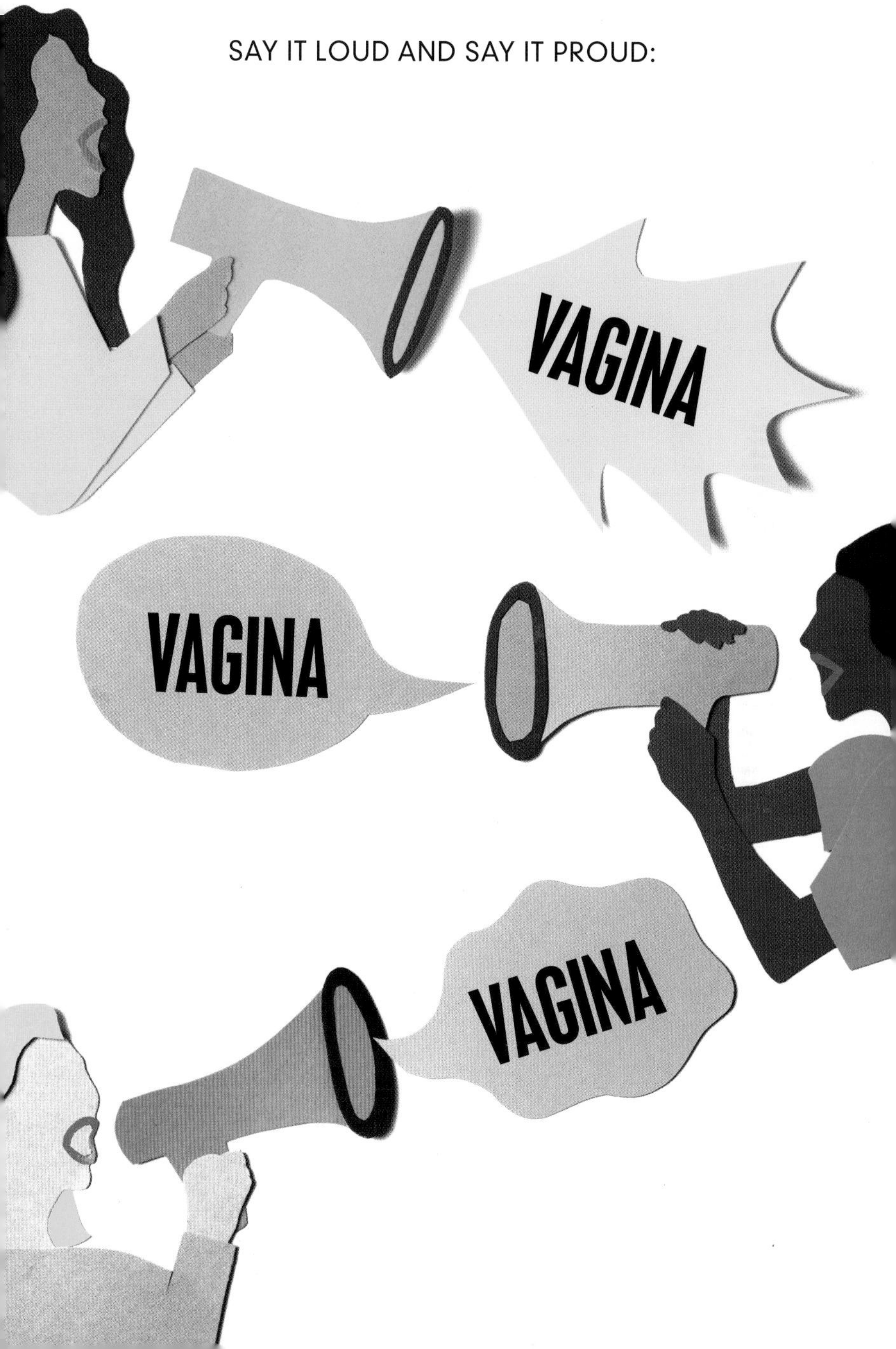

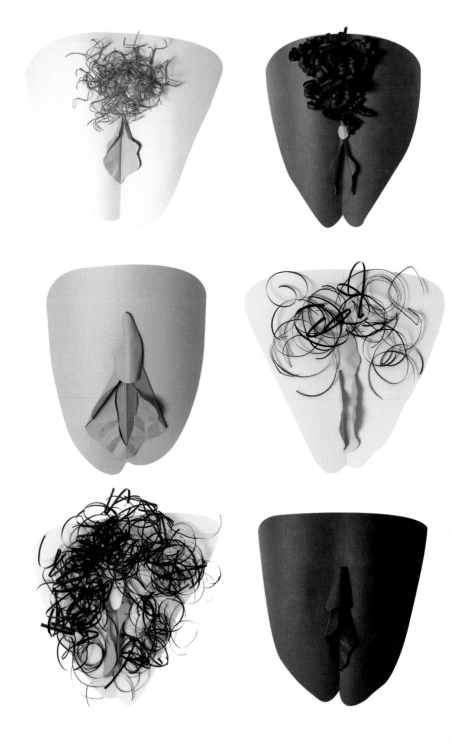

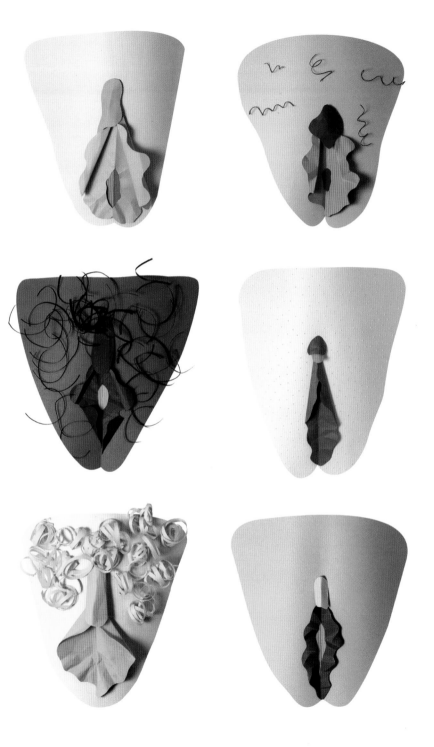

Eventually I locked the bathroom door and got a mirror out to see what exactly was going on. It looked complicated – messy and unfamiliar. After a lot of searching through medical books, I discovered that I was not the only person in the world with this crazy-looking, hairy, clam shell – I was just like every other woman out there. This complex creation we all own is often compared to a delicate and intricate flower – which I like – and since it wasn't going anywhere, I went about identifying all the parts and finding out how they worked. I discovered which bit was the clitoris (pleasure town) and which part was the urethra (pee hole). I even managed the complicated task of holding a mirror between my legs while I peed, to make sure that everything was where it was meant to be, according to the anatomy guides. Luckily it was – a relief, as I was always worried that something was going to be out of order and embarrassing.

Nowadays I don't know why we women are sometimes embarrassed about talking about our vaginas. Boys are proud of their bits! Maybe it's because ours go in and theirs go out.

54

I remember when I was about six I thought it was so unfair that boys can pee easily wherever they are, but girls can't. I was convinced that if I trained myself I could learn how to make my pee shoot out in an arc, too. I decided to give it a go. I stood a good metre away from the toilet, curled my little hips under and thrust my pee forwards, waiting for my triumphant stream to land on target in the toilet. To my horror I just felt the hot sensation of it running down my leg and into my pants around my ankles. Disappointed, I let my mum believe I'd had an 'accident'. I tried this at least five more times until I admitted defeat and felt sad about my inability to project my pee. To this day, I've never managed to get my pee to fly! (Still trying.)

Anyway, just remember: your foo foo is your friend. You will be together for life, so get to know her! KNOWLEDGE IS POWER! As soon as I felt like I knew exactly what was going on down there, I felt more confident and in control of my own body.

Here it is in all its inner glory! This diagram is EVERYTHING you need to know about your VAGIIIIIIINA! You've seen already that vaginas come in loads of different shapes, colours and sizes, but whatever yours looks like, it'll be made up of these parts.

URETHRAL OPENING (pee hole)

INNER LABIA
'Labia' just means 'lips' in Latin.
These lips surround your vagina
and urethra to protect them and
keep them clean, moist and healthy.

OUTER LABIA
These lips form the opening to your
genitals and surround your clitoris and
inner lips, protecting and enclosing them.

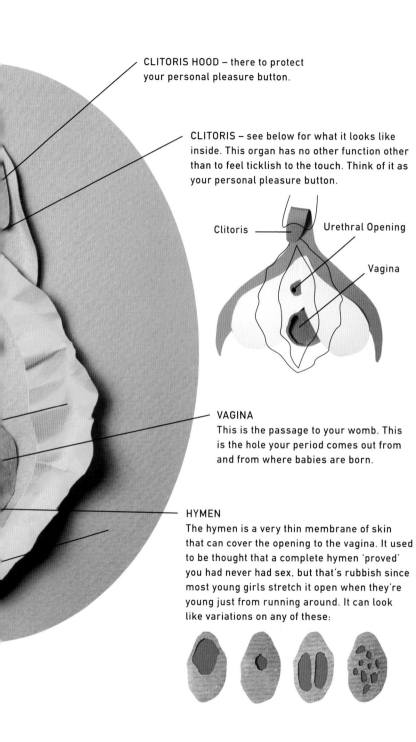

**CLITORIS HOOD** – there to protect your personal pleasure button.

**CLITORIS** – see below for what it looks like inside. This organ has no other function other than to feel ticklish to the touch. Think of it as your personal pleasure button.

Clitoris

Urethral Opening

Vagina

**VAGINA**
This is the passage to your womb. This is the hole your period comes out from and from where babies are born.

**HYMEN**
The hymen is a very thin membrane of skin that can cover the opening to the vagina. It used to be thought that a complete hymen 'proved' you had never had sex, but that's rubbish since most young girls stretch it open when they're young just from running around. It can look like variations on any of these:

# 11

# WHAT'S THE WHITE STUFF?

• • • • •

Whiteish, yellowish stuff in your knickers is 100% normal. When I first got it, I was convinced it meant there was something wrong with me but it doesn't, trust me! A healthy vagina is a moist vagina and some of that moistness gets on your knickers – that's it! Sometimes, once your periods have started, you may notice this 'discharge' looks more like a clearish jelly (actually like egg white!). This means that you are ovulating: your body has released a tiny egg and is making a nice little jelly cushion in your womb for it to land in. (I won't tell you all about how ovulation and periods work here – it's a lot to explain.) Sometimes that jelly just appears in my knickers out of nowhere, and sometimes I can feel it and I think I'm getting my period. It's weird but you get used to it! You can track it the same way you can track your periods, as it runs on the same cycle. I started putting mine into a period app which made it really easy to track. But when you first get these things they can be all over the place, so don't stress about it – just be prepared. A bit of everyday vaginal discharge is completely normal. The only time you want to investigate it is if the consistency is a bit chunkier and there is a lot of it, or if it has a really strong smell – this can be a symptom of thrush (it's treatable – see our chapter on page 198).

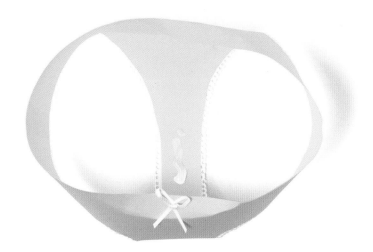

# 12

# HAIRAPY

· · · · ·

Hair is so weird. We can spend so much time banishing it from some parts of our body and then hours looking after it on other parts. And hair is magical: I have a friend who has reealllly long hair and she can actually hang from it – it's her performance specialty and it's called a 'hair suspension' – so crazy! Apart from being strong enough to hang from, our hair can also have a strong effect on how we feel – a new haircut or style can make you feel like a whole new person!

I've had so much fun with my hair – I think I've done everything: bleached it, braided it, dyed it and henna'd it. Straightened it, tied it up, slicked it back, combed it out and eventually, when nothing was left, shaved it all off (I just did it again during the making of this book, in fact)! Shaving it was cool – I felt like I was having my own personal protest against the world of

'appearance is everything'; people spend so much time worrying about how they look or what other people think of them. And the time it took to comb, style and look after a full head of my hair... I was on a mission to LIVE LIFE and spending seven or more hours a week combing and styling was not part of my plan!

So my message to you is: it's JUST HAIR – it will grow back. GO MAD, I say – EXPERIMENT. Just know that if you suddenly realise you may have made a terrible mistake with a home dying kit, or a pair of scissors and a song that made you get a little lost in the moment – it's not for ever! Embrace a haircut gone wrong and make it work for you. Add some clips, a turban, a headband, beanie, hat or wig – whatever! One day – maybe not in the near future – but one day, you will look back on that picture and laugh and laugh (and maybe remember how you cried and cried) and that will be your hair making you feel good again – hairapy rules!

# 13

# HAIR, THERE, EVERYWHERE!

• • • • •

One minute your skin is nice and smooth, the next you notice that wispy hairs have appeared under your arms and between your legs – even on your upper lip or around your nipples! It can feel like you're turning into a gorilla.

I kind of loved my new body hair and kind of hated it. At first I let it grow – it was really exciting, and a sign that I was starting to turn into a woman. But then I wanted to try taking it off too, which was also exciting. I wanted to wax, but was scared it was going to hurt. Eventually I did it and it wasn't as bad as I thought it would be. Though I did have a friend who got her bikini line waxed and it BLED a tiny bit, which put me off it for a while...

Nowadays, I think there are no rules.

64

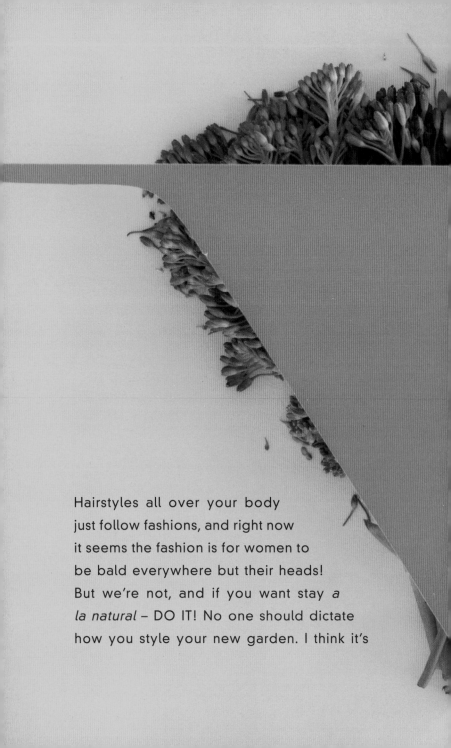

Hairstyles all over your body
just follow fashions, and right now
it seems the fashion is for women to
be bald everywhere but their heads!
But we're not, and if you want stay *a
la natural* – DO IT! No one should dictate
how you style your new garden. I think it's

beautiful, and there are loads
of women all over the world
who let their bushes and leg hair
flourish, no matter what others are
doing. If you do want to get rid of it,
that's also fine – turn to page 134 for some
hot tips.

# 14

# JUST EAT IT

· · · · ·

I ate a lot in secondary school. I figured I was growing and my body needed fuel! And grow it did... I stopped getting taller after I was about 11, but kept filling out. And I loved it – except for the stretch marks, maybe. But my mum told me those would fade, so I just hoped they would (they did) and got on with it. For breakfast in my last year of secondary school I would sometimes make a special sandwich and wash the whole thing down with a milkshake, before trying to start my day – when really all I wanted to do was go back to bed. I don't recommend this as a daily habit. I DO however recommend trying this sandwich at least once so you know what I am talking about.

Marawa's triple toastie:
– 3 slices of wholegrain bread
– 2 slices of cheese
– a tin of baked beans
– a tin of canned spaghetti

Layer the bread and cheese. In one side put the beans and in the other the spaghetti. The hardest thing is getting it into the sandwich-maker but once toasted, you are GO!

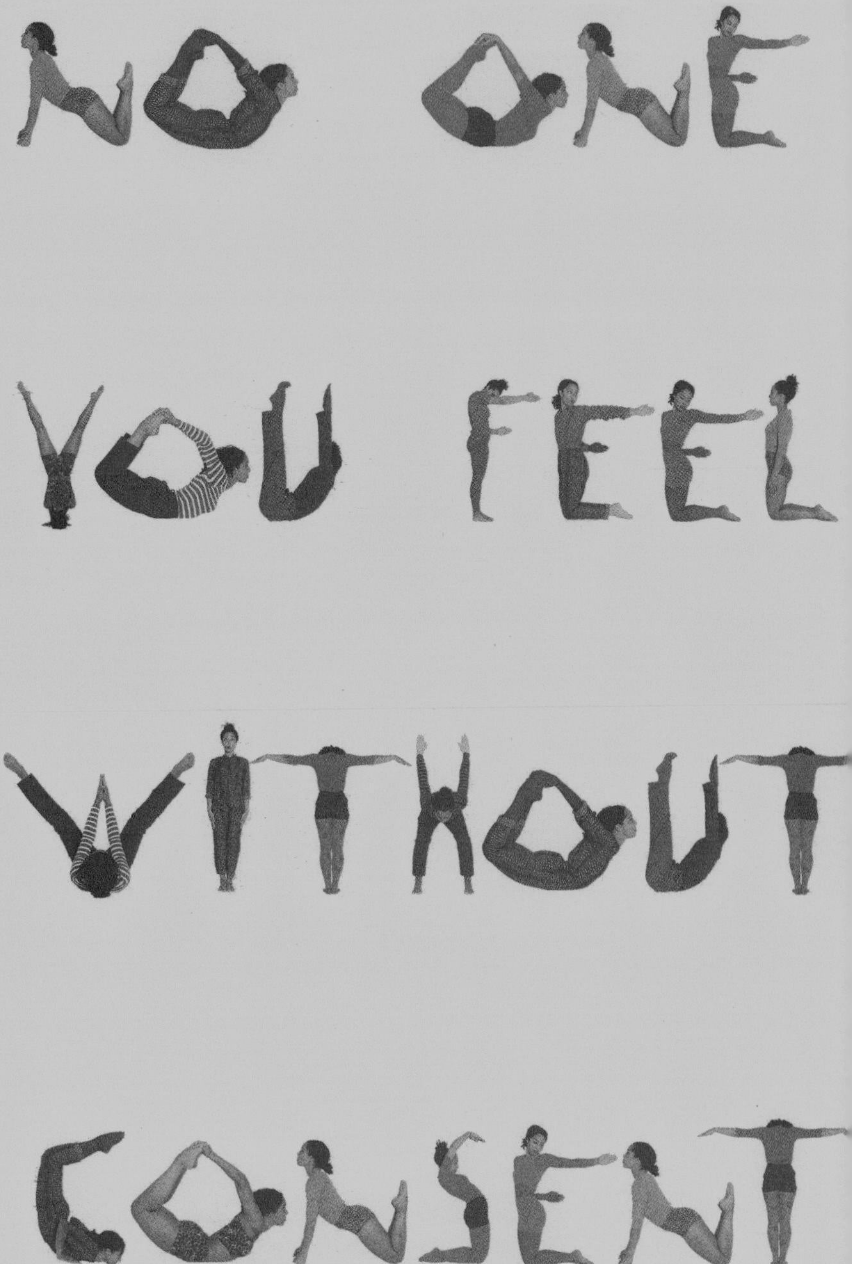

NO ONE
YOU FEEL
WITHOUT
CONSENT

CAN MAKE

INFERIOR

YOUR

— Eleanor Roosevelt

## 15

# HEARTBREAK

· · · · ·

UGH. Heartbreak HURTS. It hurts so bad you can feel like you want to dieee. But it passes – sometimes it feels like forever, but it definitely goes. Tough, tough times. I used to think it actually would hurt my heart, but it felt more like a dark cloud inside my whole body. I felt tired and heavy and I had no appetite. Everything was GREY. No one could cheer me up and I was convinced this new state of monochrome was how I would live my years out. But eventually the clouds lifted and I was able to feel happy again. All the colour of life returned and I was back to normal. The best thing to do is throw yourself into something you enjoy – do your sport; see your friends; read your books. Whatever it is, I promise it'll speed up the healing process. Distraction and time is what you need. But I completely understand your pain. ☹

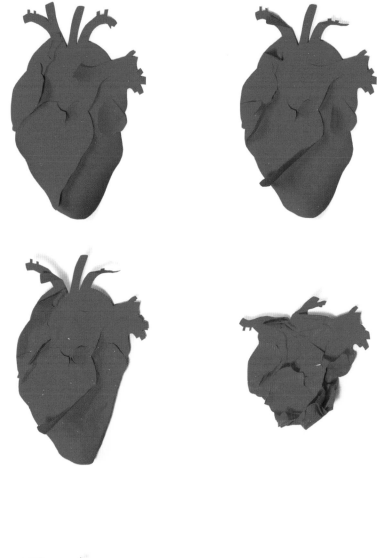

# 16

# DANCE

· · · · ·

... like nobody is watching! (Or, if you prefer, like everyone is watching!)

Sometimes a good dance can help even the biggest disaster, problem or pain. There are so many types of dance out there – jazz, ballet, contemporary, hip-hop, country, salsa, tap, line, ballroom, tango, morris, break, vogue... SO MANY – that you can take a dance class in just about anything!

A lot of dance relates to certain types of music, so that's sometimes a good way to work out what you like. Music can bring everything out of you – tears, joy, anger, energy, calmness – and moving to it is an amazing way to express your-self. You may not like what's in the charts right now, but find what works for you – there are so many great sounds out there. Experiment with the radio to find what works; what feeds your

soul. And when you find it, put it on in your bedroom and dance it out! Get your headphones out and prance around the park!

I will dance to just about anything if I like the song. I usually feel like the music takes over and I just move according to what the song is doing – it's hard to explain. I LOVE watching people dance too. Sometimes, the most unlikely people hear their tune and get so into it. You can really see a story in people's movement! My mum LOSES it anytime she hears 'I Will Survive' by Gloria Gaynor. She will drop whatever she is doing and she's off – singing; dramatic arm movements in the air; spins; wiggling fingers. It's a masterpiece! Just watching her do it makes me happy.

If you don't know where to start, just stand or sit and listen to the music. Try shaking your arms around, bending your knees in time or jumping. Not every dance needs to look like a slick music video – don't limit yourself! Find your inner dancing queen, whoever she is!

# 17

# PERIODS: THE MYSTERY

· · · · ·

Periods. Eventually they come to all of us, in various wondrous, bloody forms! Sometimes your period is heavy, sometimes light. Sometimes it comes and goes: a bit here, a bit there, nothing for a day and then it's back! But usually within a week you are safe to wear white knickers again without fear of any staining. I always need to pee more when I'm getting my period and I fart way more. Sorry, but it's true! And while I am being honest: I usually do a massive poo the day I get it. It's like my whole body is resetting, which is nice... like a monthly cleanse! Your period is just a sign that you are becoming a woman. There is nothing to be scared about, other than perhaps being stranded without a spare tampon or pad! All women have had periods throughout history: famous women, sports women, poor women, rich women – women of all religions

and all cultures in every part of the world. It's weird that we still don't hear all that much about periods – like they're something embarrassing. Thankfully, some cultures celebrate girls getting their periods, though unfortunately this is often linked to being ready for marriage and babies – which, if you still have plans for conquering the world as the best athlete, horse trainer or astronaut, might not be what you had in mind!

There are plenty of people who are comfortable talking about periods, so don't be afraid to ask questions of your friends and older girls or women. Like most things in life, with time and practice you learn how to handle them. More and more women are talking openly about their periods, sharing stories, experiences and lifting the mystery behind our monthly cycle. HURRAH!

# 18

# MY FIRST PERIOD

• • • • • •

So: my mum was in the next room with some of her friends, while all their kids, me and my brother and sister were watching TV. An advert for sanitary towels came on, with a girl smiling and riding a bike while a cute animation showed how a pad with wings would stick to your knickers. I remember thinking that riding a bike in half a nappy could NOT be comfortable. Then, a few minutes later, I suddenly felt my pants were wet. Unlike my friends – most of whom seemed to find out when they went to the toilet and found a little blood in their knickers – I knew what it was straight away. I leapt up and hurried to the toilet, squeezing like I was trying not to pee – but it made no difference and I could feel it seeping into my knickers. It didn't hurt at all – not like when you cut yourself and bleed. I just had a dull ache in my tummy. It felt so weird; I couldn't stop

it, but nor could I push it all out – it felt like my body wasn't listening to my commands.

Anyway, I sat there on the toilet trying to work out how to hide it. I really didn't want everyone to know what was going on inside my body – I wanted to deal with it myself first – but at that moment I felt very out of control. How much more blood would come? Was I going to have to sit on the toilet all night? There was no way around it – I needed my mum. I put loads of toilet paper in my pants and waddled out. She was sitting with her friends, chatting, and I called quietly to her from the doorway. She looked over to me, confused, and I said 'Mum! You need to come with me! Now!' and everyone stopped talking to look at me, which added to my already totally embarrassed state. She came, asking me what was going on, as I marched her all the way back to the bathroom. I told her I had my period and she said, 'Oh – wow – oh!' way too loudly. I was SO EMBARRASSED. Then she asked me if I was sure. I showed her my pants and then she said, 'Right, don't worry – I'll be back.' She went to the shops and came back with a huge bag of sanitary towels. Anyway, she showed me what to do and said I might want to put TWO in so that I could sleep without leaking, in case the flow stayed heavy. TWO?! These things felt ENORMOUS! I remember thinking, 'This is my life now!' Ugh!

So that was my first one, forever unforgettable. At first it felt very strange and unfamiliar. Until then, I had felt just the same as the boys I played with. Now, here was something that made me different. There was no way back and that was a weird feeling, like growing up overnight. But after all these initial panics and thoughts wore off, it got a lot better and easier! Tampons and pads went from feeling huge to tiny things you don't even notice. What had felt awkward and scary became more predictable and easy to deal with, and I learned to really appreciate how amazing my body is! Lots of girls' periods can take a couple of years to settle down and be quite irregular. Usually, they settle down, but if they don't, or if they're very heavy or painful, it's worth seeing your doctor who will be able to help.

# 19

# OWN YOUR PERIOD

· · · · · ·

Periods get a bad rap. From being called 'the curse' to whispered comments about your 'time of the month', it can seem like people only talk about the exaggerated feelings your period can bring on in a negative way. But I think there are lots of things to enjoy about your period.

In the days leading up to mine, I can feel sort of swollen all over and a bit hot. Then, when it first comes, I often get cramps in my abdomen and feel like my vagina is achey or swollen inside and out. Also, I get the occasional weird, shooty bum pain, like a muscle twitch – so weird! The cramps are annoying but I quite enjoy having a hot water bottle strapped to me and snuggling up with a cup of tea. I also have this unravelling kind of sensation, like all the tension

is leaving me. Often, halfway through my period, I feel like everything is a bit new and calm, like I'm resetting.

I used to feel really lucky to be a girl EXCEPT for periods – I thought they were so messy and gross. Having to carry tampons was annoying and it felt unfair to have to factor my period into things I did. But now I feel lucky to get it.

One thing I love about it is that my mind goes into a very productive place – I am hyper-aware of smells, sounds and touch. Things taste different – sweeter or spicier than usual – and I crave certain foods, especially potatoes. I love potatoes... The day I get my period is also my most creative: I try to draw, write or make something on this day because my mind goes to interesting places. If I'm feeling crampy, I do some stretches or go for a walk and listen to music – everything sounds good! I also feel extra-emotional – an advert on TV can make me cry – but a really good cry is such a cleansing experience! Afterwards you feel clearer in your mind as well as your sinuses... It doesn't mean you're unhappy. Then you gather yourself up, wash your face and get back to it. Getting my period lets me know my body is running smoothly. I like the monthly feeling of being very aware of myself. And I love how periods are something that bond women – we all experience the same thing and can compare notes and connect over this totally female phenomenon. Periods can feel like they are getting in the way of life but if you acknowledge what's happening, try to plan ahead and gain knowledge, you can really use your period to your advantage! Listen to your body and learn as you go: each period gives you an opportunity to see what works best for you. Don't be ruled by your period – own it.

# 20

# SANITARY SANITY

· · · · ·

In the beginning... women created sanitary towels. But this is waaaay before you could get a self-adhesive, super-absorbent, cutely-wrapped version. Before that, we had to go through all kinds of fun. Rags that were washed and reused were the most common, though poor women all over the world have also resorted to earth and even sand to catch their period – so uncomfortable! Then, around the end of the 19th century, came the 'sanitary belt' – literally a long towel that looped into hoops at the front and back on a belt around your waist. But this moved around all the time and was uncomfortable. Finally, some genius put adhesive to the underside of a pad and – VOILA! – the modern pad was born. Pad technology is always improving – pads are becoming thinner and more absorbent. Now you can even get them incorporated into the gussets of regular knickers – you can just wear... and wash!

Throughout the world, pads are still the most common method of absorbing our monthly magic. The first few days of my period are usually pretty heavy so I prefer to use tampons, but for those lighter days it's nice to have all these different options! I usually switch to a panty liner (a thin pad) or the all-in-one knickers.

And know this: all of us, many times, have had to roll up toilet paper to make an emergency pad. And it always – without fail – works its way up the back of your knickers as you walk. And sometimes even out the top. It's okay! We've all been there!

Sanitary towel checklist:

- Keep one or two handy: the 'emergency pad' in my bag has saved me many times!
- Work out how to stick it in the middle – which is usually over your gusset. At night, if you sleep on your back, you will want to stick it further towards the back of your pants (and vice versa for front/ side sleeping). Or try a night-time pad – they are longer!
- Dispose of them properly! Wrap the old one up with toilet paper or the wrapper of your next pad and make sure it is fully in the bin, rather than sticking to the lid! Also, never flush them – no one wants to swim in the ocean with your used pad. Trust me.
- Just like tampons and menstrual cups, you need to change your pad regularly – usually a few times a day, depending on how heavy your flow is and how absorbent it is.

| PROS: | CONS: |
|---|---|
| ● You can see everything, and know when you need to change. | ● They can chafe and feel uncomfortable! You can't forget you're on your period like with tampons and menstrual cups. |
| ● Nothing to learn – tampons and menstrual cups take a bit of practice, so pads are a great place to start. | ● You can't swim – and I love swimming! |
| | ● Sometimes, the sticky back catches on your pubic hairs. Ouch! |

# 21

# TAMPONS – THE THING ON THE STRING

· · · · ·

I used to think that tampons just kind of sat outside of you long-ways – like a pad but without sticking to your knickers. I was SO HORRIFIED when I found out it had to go INSIDE you – I could not wrap my head around it. It seemed so messy and dirty and gross. When I finally got my period, I tried pads but I couldn't deal with them – I was always leaking and it felt like a giant surfboard in my pants. So I spent a whole afternoon jamming tampons up inside me to try them out. At first I only put each one JUST inside me – I didn't understand that you had to push it up further, and anyway I was worried it would just go up and not come back out. But it was soooo uncomfortable… I walked around with it grating inside me and it just felt horrible. Eventually I worked out that if you push it up higher then you won't be able to feel it anymore. Hurrah! Also, even if the string accidentally goes up, too, you can still get to it – it's just a li'l fiddly! Once I worked tampons out I never looked back: I was back to swimming, running, jumping – everything!

Interesting fact: even though woman-kind has done well fighting for equality over the years, there is such a thing as 'tampon tax' – proof that we still have a bit of work to do. Tampons (and all sanitary products, like pads and menstrual cups) are classed by the govern-ment as 'luxury' items. In other words, they're something you want but don't really *need*, and so have to pay more for. Excuse me? In what way are sanitary products 'non-essential' items? This drives me CRAZY! There have been so many discussions about removing the tax but as I write these words, women still have to pay to have periods. Unbelievable.

Tampon checklist:

Don't leave it in too long and read the packaging to make sure you're wearing the right size. It's POSSIBLE (but highly unlikely) that you might get a reaction to it, called Toxic Shock Syndrome.

Try to buy natural ones. A number of tampons contain things other than plain cotton. Read the labels and ask!

Carry spares in your bag. You can easily disguise them so they don't fall out everywhere when you take out your bus pass. Find a cute little tin or make-up bag.

Help your fellow sister. I have been saved by, or helped, many a girl with a spare tampon when a period turned up – especially at first, when your cycle can be a bit of a mystery!

Don't flush them – just like pads, you need to dispose of them in the bin.

| PROS: | CONS: |
|---|---|
| ● You can swim! | ● If you don't change your tampon in time you can leak into your knickers. |
| ● You can't feel it once it has been inserted properly, unlike a pad. | ● They take a little practice to get used to. |
| ● They're small and easy to carry around. | ● If your flow is too light to soak into the whole tampon, it can grate when you pull it out. |

# 22

# CUP O' MOON

· · · · · ·

Menstrual cups, known more commonly by their brand name 'Moon Cups' are not as well-known as tampons and pads, but are becoming super popular as they are reusable and environmentally friendly. A menstrual cup is small and made of latex rubber – you kind of fold it in half lengthways and then insert it into your vagina. Once inside, it pops open and is held there by the walls of your vagina. It creates a cup that catches the blood rather than soaking it up like a tampon would. Then, when you want to change it, you pull it out by the nozzle at the bottom, tip it into the toilet bowl (making beautiful patterns against the white porcelain), rinse it and pop it back in again. It can take a while to get used to but there are loads of tutorials online that show how to insert one, and once you've got the hang of it, you and your menstrual cup can go anywhere and everywhere together!

Menstrual cup checklist:

Get a size that works for you – the first one I tried was too big and I couldn't get comfortable at all! You may need to try different brands.

Even though it holds three times as much liquid as a tampon, you are still meant to empty it out every 4–6 hours. You need to make sure your hands are really clean when using your menstrual cup.

It's one of the trickier things to get the hang of, so read up and learn as much as you can through other people's stories first.

Read the cup's cleaning instructions carefully.

| PROS: | CONS: |
|---|---|
| • You only have to buy it once! No more running to the shop because you've run out of tampons/pads. Also because of this, it's super eco-friendly! | • It can be messy! Especially if it is quite full – you need to really practise removing the cup a few times to be able to do it neatly. |
| • It holds a lot of flow so you can leave it in a little longer than a tampon and – like a tampon – you can't feel a thing. So you can completely forget you're on your period all day at school. | • It can be difficult to empty out in a public toilet because you need to wash your hands and rinse the cup. The trick is to take a bottle of water in with you. |
| • You see everything! Emptying a menstrual cup is an amazing insight into what is going on inside your body! A lot of girls have made art using the menstrual blood to create amazing pictures. | • It's tricky to insert at first. It requires a bit of practice to get the fold and insertion right. But once you've got it, you'll never look back! |

# THE LEAK STORY

· · · · ·

When I first got my period, I read up on everything I could about this new mystery thing. One of the things I 'learned' (and later found to be completely useless) is that periods run on a 28-day cycle – so I marked down a huge red 'P' every 28th day in my diary and thought that was that taken care of. A couple of months later, we went out for a day trip with another family. There were lots of kids, including a teenage boy the same age as me. We had a great day out and then everyone piled back in the cars to go home again and lots of the kids wanted to travel together in one car. So I was wedged between my brother and this other boy my age, and I suddenly realised I was getting my

102

period. I was horrified. Not only did we have a loooong car journey ahead of us, but because I knew this was a day I was NOT MEANT to get my period, I dressed that morning in my white denim dungarees. Can you believe it? With an orange tie-dyed t-shirt, if I remember correctly. I panicked and clenched my legs hard, trying to stop any from coming out of me – but every now and then I felt it trickling out, no matter how hard I squeezed! I was trying to act like nothing was happening and laughed away but that only made it worse – every time I laughed I felt more coming out of me. At one point I casually looked down to try to check between my legs and see if it was real or if it was all in my mind (y'know, the way you think it's everywhere when actually it's just a tiny spot on your knickers?) and, Lord almighty, there was UNDENIABLE, BRIGHT RED-AS-RED BLOOD SOAKING THROUGH MY WHITE-AS-WHITE DENIM DUNGAREES!

Then a new panic set in – what about the seat? Was it all over the seat? Did it smell? I was mortified. I was horrified at the thought that this boy was going to see it. I felt so exposed and gross. I just figured I had to keep my legs as tightly together as possible and go straight into the house when we got back. When we fiiinally got home, I had to get out before the boy and do this kind of weird pigeon walk out of the car, tucking my bum under because I was convinced that was the only way he wouldn't see. I don't know whether it worked. At last, I got back to the safety of my room, but that was still only halfway – because then there was the clean up. Were my fabulous white dungarees ever going to be white again? I tried desperately to work out whether hot water or cold water was going to get this stain out, filling a big bowl with every type of cleaning product I could find (for future reference, always use COLD WATER!). Then I hid my sorry -looking dungarees in the wash basket and hoped for the best. But they were never the same again. They would forever be as stained as my memory of this day AND my confidence

in my period calendar! Suddenly this so-called 'curse of womanhood' all made sense and it made me feel depressed...

Anyway, I am so grateful now for my period app, which lets me know pretty accurately when it is coming. Although I know not to be surprised if it's a day or two either side and that things like stress and travel can cause it to break its regular pattern altogether and just show up. Which is what happened to me AGAIN only the other day when I was wearing – wait for it – white jeans! I went to get lunch but it was a really long walk and just as I got to the shop I realised I had started bleeding. I felt pretty confident that I wasn't going to bleed through, because I am, of course, 'old and mature' now and know my body so much better, so I picked up my lunch and walked all the way back to this theatre where I was performing that night. But when I got to the bathroom I was in exactly the same state as I had been twenty years ago. The only difference was that this time I was far less embarrassed. And luckily, I had a change of clothes!

INHALE

EXHALE

# 24

# GENERATION OLD

· · · · ·

I was around thirteen when my parents started irritating me. Literally every single thing they said was annoying. It took a few years till that went away and now my mum is my #1! I am always so excited to talk to her and tell her what I have been doing – she is always there to listen to me and I appreciate it so much. Being a mum must be so intense – I don't know how she did it; I am amazed when I think about it. Giving up all your time to look after someone else. I am forever grateful! But for a while there I thought she was desperately uncool and I was not interested in ANYTHING she had to say. Parents (or whoever looks after you) sticking their nose in when you don't want them around is the worst... embarrassing you in front of your friends, having NO IDEA what good music sounds like or why one pair of trainers is 50,000 times better than a no-brand, cheaper pair.

But the thing is, they have done all of this themselves! They were young once; they went through school and sweaty years and will have great tips and ideas from their own experiences. Letting them pass these on to you could even make for some good bonding. My mum was my biggest source of information for all things body-related and I would ask her EVERYTHING. She always had a story about something that had happened to her that was similar to whatever I was feeling. The fact is, the clothes, music and technology might change, but people's experiences stay pretty much the same.

At the end of the day, even when I was embarrassed of her, I knew deep down that she was the best. She brought me into this world and gave me the opportunity to LIVE! That's something that can never be changed and I've always felt pretty grateful. So – give generation old a chance. I promise you, they're doing their best!

THERE IS NO
LIKE THAT
TWO WOMEN
CHOSEN TO

INTIMACY

BETWEEN

WHO HAVE

BE SISTERS.

— Warsan Shire

# 25

# VIRTUAL REALITY

. . . . .

Make-up is super fun. I love it as much as the next showgirl and it's such a great way to experiment with different looks, themes, styles and how you're feeling on a certain day. But when it becomes a mask that you can't leave the house without wearing, you need to pause and think about why you are doing it. Are you trying to disguise the way you really look? Are you aspiring to the impossible? Because the fact is, Photoshop is everywhere. You can't trust anything you see! That perfect bikini body? That flawless face? Everything we see online or in print is retouched. There is no point comparing yourself with what you see in magazines – E-V-E-RY-THING is retouched and has been altered in some way – like teeth being made whiter and of course skin made tighter. Women have been looking at magazines and billboards

114

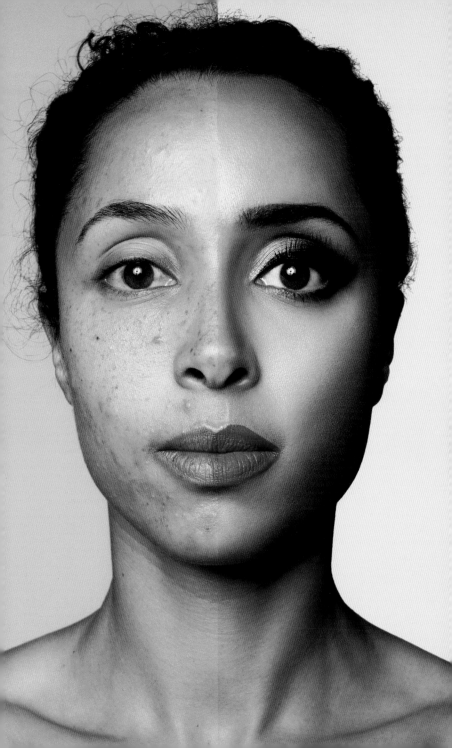

for years, comparing themselves to figures they believe to be 'ideal' or examples of 'perfection' that are not even REAL PEOPLE! Don't compare yourself to magazines. In fact, cross out 'comparing' off your list altogether! Comparing yourself to anyone is a sure-fire way to make you feel bad about yourself. We are all different, and there are beautiful and lovable things about all of us that a retouched image can never hope to express. Whatever your face, whatever your shape, embrace it, love it, cover it in moisturiser, stretch it out and don't lose touch with it. Society and the media have taken it so far that we are now finding ways to recreate Photoshop in real life – using products on our skin with names such as 'photo finish'! It's so crazy, right?! Rise above all the trashy magazines and know that a girl who likes herself, looks good. Period.

# 26

# FEED YOUR BRAIN

· · · · · ·

Your brain is like a muscle, and like all muscles, it needs STIMULATION to stay fit. You need to keep feeding and exercising it! And you really need to think about WHAT you are feeding it. You wouldn't eat chocolate bars for every meal and expect your body to work to its full potential – in the same way you don't want to feed your brain uninspiring trash!

The internet is an amazing source of stimulation, but the way we use it can get really stale. You end up looking at the same clips, hearing the same songs, playing the same games... Switching things up will exercise your brain and lead you to new places. Every so often, check out new websites, with your parents' permission of course. Look up a question you might have; search for events or people you're interested in; or find blogs for hobbies you'd like to try.

There's a whole world out there, but we often just stick to the same little bits we know. I like to make myself listen to music I wouldn't normally listen to – even if I hate it! I try to listen to the whole song to see how it makes me feel by the end, or what sort of images it creates in my mind. Sometimes I reimagine music videos for songs I like – music is a great way to let your imagination go somewhere new.

And while in one sense the internet can take you anywhere without even leaving your house, the truth is you are just sitting, looking at a lit-up screen. It's hard to stay away from technology – for adults, too – but getting out into the real world and seeing and doing things is a completely different experience to hunching over a tablet or laptop. Be open to new things, even if you think they might be boring. Learn a card trick, pick up a book you wouldn't usually read or make a model aeroplane! Keep exploring wherever you go – fill your brain with the best quality ideas, challenges, images, sounds and colours!

NOTHING WILL WORK

start

end

UNLESS YOU DO

— Maya Angelou

# 27

# IF ONLY...

· · · · · ·

'If only' is that tiny voice in your head telling you that if only you had a smaller nose/ shinier hair/ longer legs, then everything would be okay.

Everyone experiences wanting what they don't have at some point in life. But when it's about your body it can feel harder: it can be tied up with how much you value yourself and think other people value you. 'If only' is TOXIC. It means you're never satisfied, here and now. The fact is, your legs probably aren't going to get longer, BUT you have loads of other amazing things about you. And – trust me – liking your-self and your own shape is the most attractive quality anyone can have. Sometimes, when I was younger I would catch myself thinking that if only I'd been born in the 1950s, or lived in a differ-ent country, my body shape would have been more 'right'. But eventually I realised the most

appealing thing about another person is when they are comfortable in their own skin. Sooooo much easier said than done – but really – it's true.

It also seems so crazy to want to be a particular way when there are so many different ideas of beauty right now all over the world. I travel a LOT, and it seems so nuts to me that in countries where most women have dark skin, the supermarket shelves are filled with dangerous bleaching creams to make their complexion lighter – whilst women in other parts of the world with white skin risk skin cancer by baking themselves under sunbeds or getting oiled up at the beach, in pursuit of a 'healthy' tan.

So, take a minute to stop giving yourself such a hard time and take a look at yourself. What's nice about you? What DO you like? What would you never change? Congratulate yourself on these things! Write them down if you want. Then, when you feel the IF ONLYs coming back, read them again and remind yourself that you have a lot of qualities that are GREAT! Give yourself a high-five in the mirror and smile!

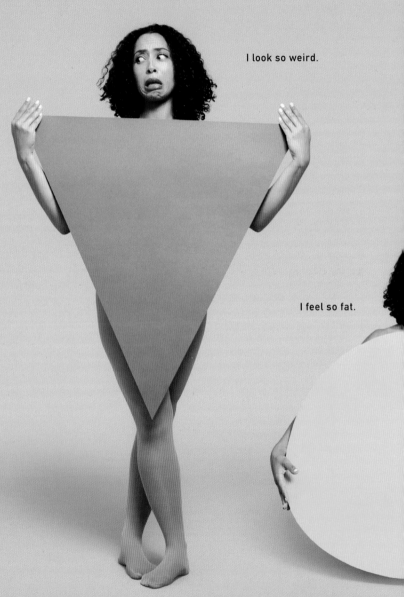

Urgh, my shoulders
are so wide,

so pointy.

I look so weird.

I feel so fat.

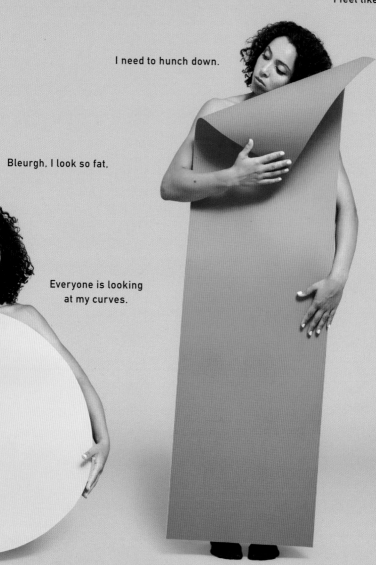

Yes, look at my great shape!

I love my tummy.

So sharp!

Loving my angles.

I'm a curvy crusader!

# 28

# STRETCH MARKS

· · · · · ·

Stretch marks can happen and if they do, there is no way around 'em. They are annoying but they fade. They come up in places where you are E-X-P-A-N-D-I-N-G and the skin has to stretch quickly to accommodate your new body. I got them on my legs, my bum and all over my new boobs. They can be pretty scary at first and can be anything from skin-coloured to pink or purple. I was SO UPSET when I saw them coming up all over my boobs like spider webs – I thought I would never be able to wear a round-necked top. But eventually I did! You just have to get over it and own them. Some girls really celebrate their stretch marks now, which is GREAT – you can't avoid them so you might as well embrace them!

---

FACT: If you lather yourself in moisturiser every day you can reduce stretch marks. But just know that most will fade over time.

---

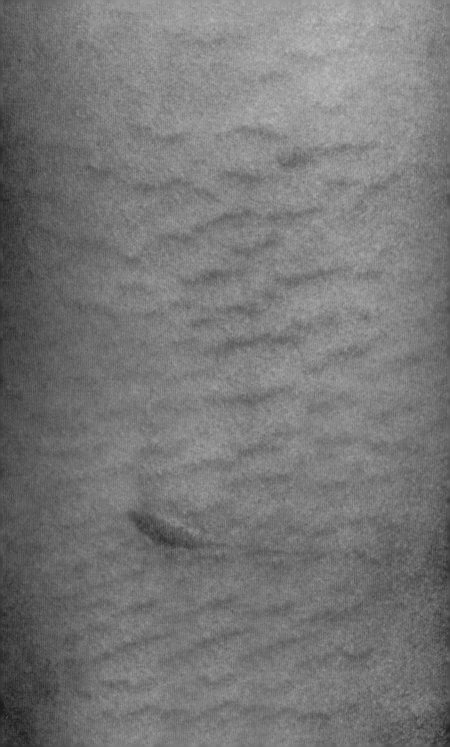

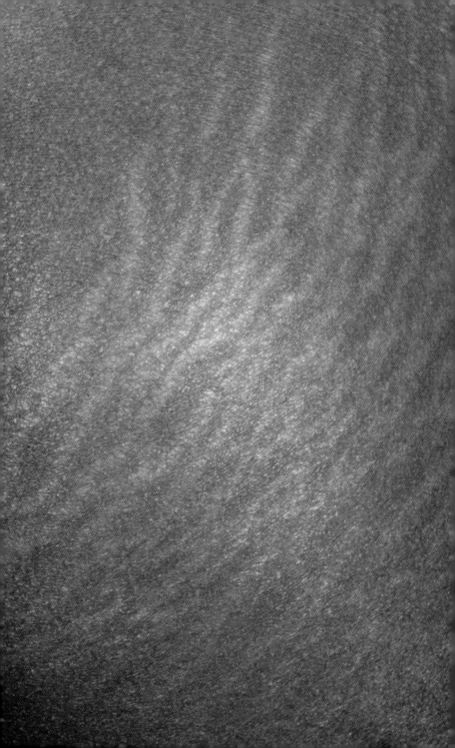

# HAIR TODAY, GONE TOMORROW

• • • • •

If you decide there are bits of your body you want hair-free, here's the low-down:

 Trimming

This is removing the hair from where it grows out of the skin. Because you are snipping it half way up (each hair has a root beneath the skin, like a plant!) the hair can grow back looking thicker. But it's the cheapest and easiest DIY route.

SHAVING: mind the sharp blades; please don't cut yourself! Also make sure you do it with wet legs – the first time I did it was with dry legs and it was so itchy. Afterwards, moisturise your skin.

HAIR-REMOVAL CREAMS: buy at a chemist, put it on the hair and it... melts it. It's quick and easy, though I don't like to think what those chemicals are doing to your skin.

PROS: quick, cheap, with total smoothness at first.

CONS: possible rash and scratchy regrowth stubble after a day or two.

## Plucking

Yes, like a chicken. I mean pulling the hair out from its root (ouch!) so that when it grows back it's soft, not stubbly. You do have to make sure it's long enough before you can do it again, though – which can be annoying if the party is on Saturday but the hair is so short that it won't be ready to wax before Tuesday...

WAXING: expensive at the salon, messy at home. Wax strips are easiest, but be careful not to let them touch anything other than you – it's impossible to get the wax off. Press one on, then whip it off fast, like a giant plaster – yeeouch!

THREADING: a beautician runs twisted string along the skin, plucking out any hair along the way. It's not one to try without a professional, but there are loads of threading salons everywhere or stands in department stores and chemists.

EPILATORS: a little machine you can buy, which has whirring discs that spin next to one another, catching your hairs as you pass it over them and whipping 'em out. These don't cost much more than a wax at the salon but they last for years.

| PROS: lasts for weeks with soft regrowth. |
| --- |
| CONS: hurts a little; costs a little more; sometimes the hairs get stuck under your skin when they're growing back and cause spots and in-grown hairs. |

137

## 30

# I ♥ THE WORD FAT!

· · · · · ·

Fat gets a bad rep in the press. You HAVE to have some, even if it's just a bit – it's essential to living! Some of us just have those jelly genes that make us put on extra weight as we get womanly curves – it's completely normal. In general, getting chubby didn't bother me too much – I felt like I ate really well and did a lot of exercise, so at first I was confused when I started putting on weight. I thought maybe I was doing something wrong. But you can be totally healthy and have some wobble and jelly on you, too! You are getting taller and growing boobs 'n' things, so extra weight elsewhere is going to happen. It can feel heavy and if it happens quickly, your clothes can suddenly feel tight but don't worry – it means you're becoming a woman. So embrace thy thighs! Fat is fun! It keeps you warm! Plus every seat is comfortable. Work out what to wear to make yourself feel good and over time your curves will feel more familiar. Don't panic if it feels like a shock at first – it is a really big thing to get used to a new body shape!

That said, don't let putting on weight hold you down – literally. You want to resist falling into the 'I'm sooo bored and tired; I've got my period; leave me alone I will eat this whole packet of choc-chip biscuits if I feel like it' mode – that will probably just leave you feeling bad about yourself. Sure, every now and then we need to chill, but you also need to be getting a good amount of exercise. Build those muscles! Exercise may start to feel like your enemy – when I put on weight, I suddenly hated running – but I still enjoyed trampolining and roller skating. You have to do what feels right for you, whether it's tennis, yoga, football, t'ai chi – whatever. Instead of trying to control and suppress your new body, see how you can work with it. Try to focus on what you can do to help your body and make it grow STRONG.

31

DO NOT BECOME A STRANGER TO YOURSELF BY BLENDING IN WITH

144

EVERYONE

ELSE

— Dodinsky

## 32

# CH–CH–CH–

• • • • •

Something happened to me one summer, when I was about 12. My body was filling out and getting rounder and suddenly, one day, every step caused my inner thighs to rub together where they met! Before I had even made it ten steps out of the house it felt like I had an irritated hot red patch of chafed thigh at the top of my leg. OUCH!

To stop it happening, I used to wear cotton cycling shorts under my school uniform every

# CH—CHAFING!

day. This probably didn't help when I had thrush (see page 198), since they were tight and no doubt made me sweatier, but it definitely helped my legs glide past one another without rubbing. Sweaty summer legs are the perfect way to end up with a whole LOT of chafe! If your legs start to rub together, try to remember when you're getting dressed in the morning so you don't get caught out!

# 33

# BUMS

· · · · ·

I love my bum – always have. When I was young, it was bigger and big bums were not fashionable. In those days, the 'waif' look was in – pretty much just skin and bone. But I still loved my bum! It was like a personal cushion and a very useful muscle for running and dancing. The only thing that has ever annoyed me about it is that NO TROUSERS FITTED. EVER. If I could get my legs into them, there would be a huge gap at the waist, or if the waist fitted then they would be so tight round my thighs that I couldn't move. The only ones I ever found that fitted were vintage ones from a charity shop, made in the 1950s. These trousers seemed to understand the curves of a woman – because that was the shape that was fashionable then. They were tailored to go out at the thigh and hip and then come back in at the waist. Now I look at skinny jeans and know there is NO WAY my leg – let alone my arm! – is going to fit in that. It seems so unfair that all these trousers are designed for the latest shape, when most of the population look nothing like that! Millions of women try to cram themselves into a fabric cage and then feel bad because their beautiful bodies don't fit!

And don't talk to me about knickers – sheesh... For years I had a permanent wedgie! I would put them on, take three steps and they would be up my bum. I tried everything: boy leg, bloomer, low rise, fuller cut... hungry bum 100%. I would have to go to the toilet just to un-wedge myself, pull my knickers down as low as possible and hope that they would stay there until I was at least back in class – it was so uncomfortable! Finally, I made my own pants – my friend worked in fashion and we made a pair of wedge-proof knickers. I spent weeks testing them out until we found the perfect design that would stay PUT! So I say LOVE your bum, look after it and dress it so that it looks its best, regardless of fashion!

## 34

# FEELING HOT-HOT-HOT

· · · · · ·

Sometimes it can feel like sex is everywhere – that everyone is doing it and everything is pointing towards it. True, without it none of us would be here, but over the last hundred years or so sex has gone from being a subject that was barely acknowledged in public to being the #1 way of advertising just about anything, from deodorant to spaghetti. It's in music videos, it's on billboards and it's confusing! Why is that woman making bedroom eyes while holding a piece of celery? Is she advertising a juicing machine or... what, exactly?

So, before you have even had sex you will already have been bombarded with images that suggest sexy things – which is weird, right?! And – for all the juice-press commercials and sexy music videos – there is very little out there about actual real sex. SO much of what you see is nothing like the real thing and looks more like two people putting on a show than really enjoying themselves. Imagine a TV programme with really, really bad acting, where all the conversation just seems totally awkward and fake – it's the same deal. And it's weird because, although sex is out there THE WHOLE TIME on TV and in adverts, people get embarrassed talking about it, so there's no one to let you know that it's not like that at all. What's a girl to do?

Well, while it's totally normal to feel interested in sex and how it feels, my advice is to wait until you're older and with someone you're TOTALLY relaxed with. There is no perfect time to lose your virginity and no rules about who, how, what, where and when, but your virginity – like your body – is yours and only you get to decide what you do with it. You want to be comfortable and safe enough to explore your own desires. And in the meantime, feel free to do some exploring on your own! Your body is 100% yours, so enjoy it!

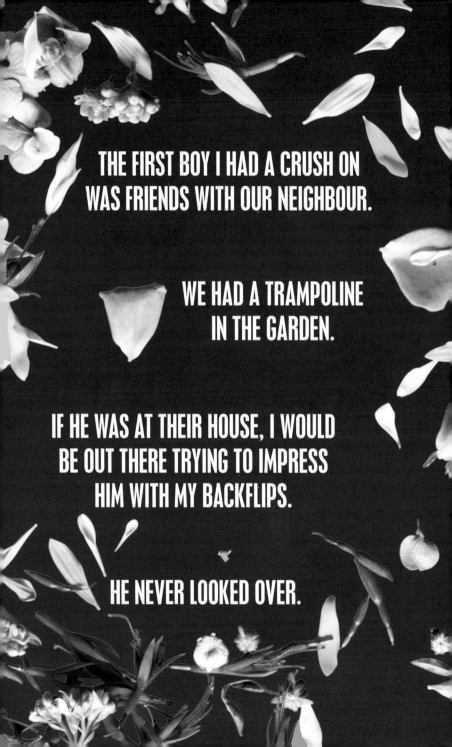

THE FIRST BOY I HAD A CRUSH ON
WAS FRIENDS WITH OUR NEIGHBOUR.

WE HAD A TRAMPOLINE
IN THE GARDEN.

IF HE WAS AT THEIR HOUSE, I WOULD
BE OUT THERE TRYING TO IMPRESS
HIM WITH MY BACKFLIPS.

HE NEVER LOOKED OVER.

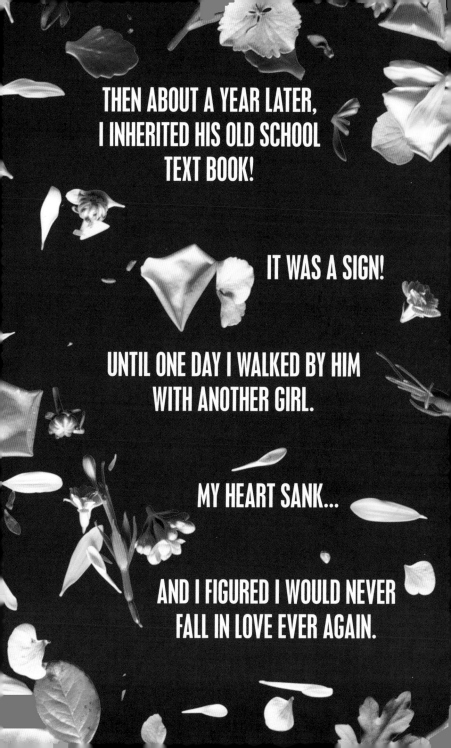

THEN ABOUT A YEAR LATER,
I INHERITED HIS OLD SCHOOL
TEXT BOOK!

IT WAS A SIGN!

UNTIL ONE DAY I WALKED BY HIM
WITH ANOTHER GIRL.

MY HEART SANK...

AND I FIGURED I WOULD NEVER
FALL IN LOVE EVER AGAIN.

# 35

# TIDAL MOODS AND HOR-MOANS

· · · · ·

I am really into the moon – any time I start feeling crazy I check the calendar and it's usually around full-moon time. It's really not just an old wives tale! The Moon has a huge effect on the ocean – it controls the tides, and since our bodies are made up of 65% water, it makes sense that we have our own tides, too, sometimes high and sometimes low.

Anyway, emotions get a bit crazier when hormones start hanging out at PU-BER-TY. I could go from normal Marawa to stone-faced, 'DO NOT TALK TO ME OR I WILL PUNCH YOU SO HARD YOU WON'T WAKE UP TILL CHRISTMAS' Marawa in a nanosecond, just because someone had looked at me a bit funny. And sometimes, when my mum asked me for the tenth time, 'What

I love
everybody!

is wrong? Do you want a cup of tea?' I would storm off screaming to my room and then when I got there, not be entirely sure what was wrong myself. But I would stick to my mood for at least an hour or two – just to be consistent.

Meanwhile, your friends are all doing it, too! One minute they are cool, the next they are whispering around you and giving you blank looks – then they're your best friend again. Ugh. It's really a full-time job keeping up with all of this – let alone getting homework done.

So what's my advice? Be kind. Your feelings are real, of course! But maybe you don't have to really take them out on everyone else. Looking back, I could have said, 'I'm just feeling a bit off today, Mum, I don't know why. And NO – thank you – NO tea.'

Sometimes when I am in that zone I can actually tell it's happening, and try really hard not to take it out on others. The best thing about this is that you become aware that maybe your friend who is being weird is just having an off day too!

# 36

# PASS THE PARACETAMOL

• • • • • •

No one wants to be in pain – why would they? Then again, there are loads of different types – some are just the daily aches of being a human. Like growing pains – my knees used to hurt SO MUCH, my mum would give me two hot water bottles to wrap around them. And period pain – at school, girls would always ask to go to the teacher for some paracetamol at the first sign. It's easy to start relying on painkillers but, over time, it's not great to be putting them into your body all the time. Stretching can be a great alternative for helping relieve headaches, period pain, stomach and muscle pain. Try some of the stretches on the following pages before you reach for the pills...

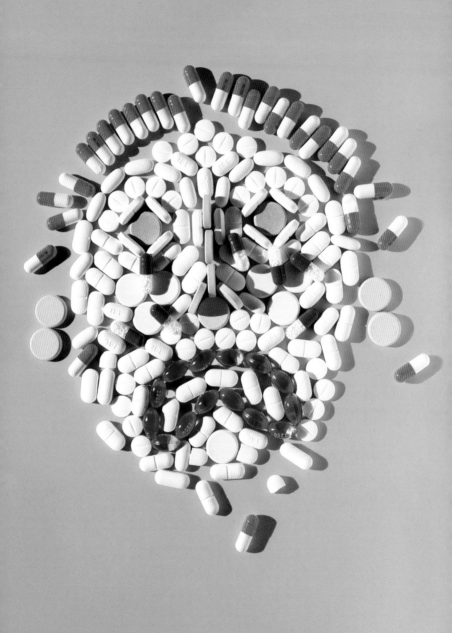

# 37

# STRE-E-E-E-ETCH

• • • • •

Stretching makes you feel gooood. It sends fresh blood flowing into your muscles, warming them up and helping them relax. It helps relieve tension in your body, like period pain or a sore neck and – over time – it improves your flexibility. One thing: it's important not to over-stretch and push harder when it already hurts. Be patient – find a stretch that feels only a little bit uncomfortable and then focus on your breathing, taking long, deep breaths in and out and staying in the stretch as long as you can (60 seconds is ideal). In fact, practising deep breathing is key! You can really relax and calm your mind and body through deep, regular breaths – try it!

## KNOTTY NECK

Stand with your back against the wall and then gently sink your head forward until you've got a really good double chin. Take a deep breath and come back out. Then gently tilt your head to one side, so you feel a stretch across the opposite side of your neck. Take a deep breath and come back to the centre. Repeat on the other side. Never roll your neck around in full circles – always come back to looking straight ahead between each stretch.

## TIGHT SHOULDERS

If you're on the computer too much or even texting a lot, sometimes your shoulders can get really tight. To release some tension, try bringing your shoulders right up to your ears – squeeze them up! Then drop and relax them. Repeat five or six times! You can also swing your arms around your body and shake it out, shake it out! This will help loosen up your shoulders.

## NO-FUN
## KNEES

I remember growing pains in my knees – yeeouch! Stretch your calves by standing on a step and letting your heels drop down low, or try doing little knee circles with your hands on your knees and your feet together. Resting an ankle on the opposite knee and letting your knee fall out to the side also feels good. Even just lying down with your feet raised on a cushion can help the blood flow.

## BAD
## BACK

With bent knees and your feet together, try bending over to touch your toes – this is a really good one to stretch out your lower back. From here you can also walk on the spot to really feel it in each hip and on each side. Then – I love this – lie on your back, bring your knees up to your chest and hug them. Then rock from side-to-side. Great for period pain.

## CHURNING STOMACH

Lie on your back with your palms facing up, your legs relaxed and toes falling outwards. Breathe deeply and imagine you are breathing into your belly button – making it push out. Don't use your muscles to push out, though, let the air do it! Once you are breathing deeply, count 10 breaths or 20 if you have time! This will really help you relax.

## HUNCHY HANDS

Start by stretching all your fingers out as far as you can – and holding that for 10-20 seconds. Put all your fingers together and point them down towards your wrist, to stretch out the back of your hand. Then, put your hands together in a prayer position and bring your elbows up, keeping your wrists together to stretch the front of your wrist.

## PERIOD PAINS

'Child's pose' is my favourite period pain-relief pose: you kneel on the floor, sitting on your ankles, and then stretch your arms up high as you breathe in. Then, exhale and stretch your arms out far in front, with your forehead on the ground. You can stay here for ages – don't fall asleep! It is really relaxing and helps to relieve stomach cramps.

## HIP, HIP HOORAY!

This is amazing for stretching out your legs but also taking pressure off your lower back. Make sure your knee is on something soft. Then, think about tucking your hips under so that you get a great stretch along the front of your leg and hip. Try to stay there for three deep breaths. Then, straighten your front leg and stretch your hamstring out, too!

# 38

# MEDITAAAAAATION

· · · · ·

Phones, computers, school, friends, family... everything! Sometimes it all gets a bit much and your head feels kind of full. Sometimes you just need to take 10–20 minutes to RESET. And the good news is that you can! Anywhere! At home, in your room, in the bathroom – wherever. Here is how I like to take a li'l break:

Turn everything off – phone, laptop, music... even the lights if you want. You can lie, sit, have your eyes open or closed. Whatever works for you – this is YOUR time.

Now. Think about your breathing and nothing else. Try to make your mind like a clear blue sky. Thoughts will come, but try to let them just pass through your mind like clouds that you watch until they are gone, leaving your mind clear and blue again. Listen to your breath going in and out. Try to breathe as deeply as possible,

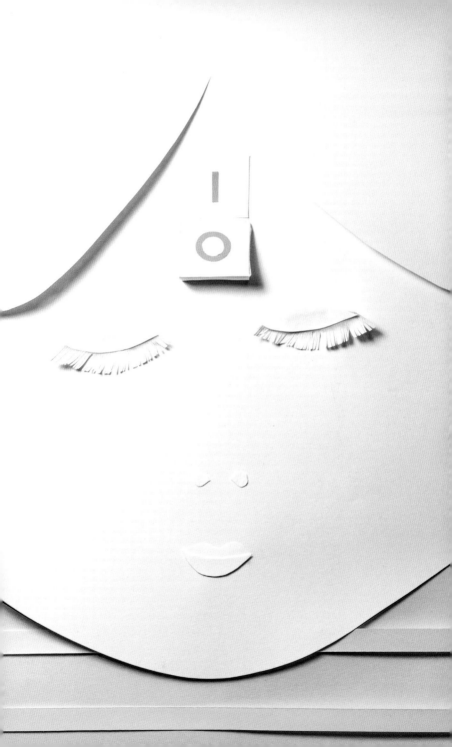

letting your tummy relax and expand with each breath. If you feel your mind wandering off, thinking about something you wish you hadn't said, or how your red jumper would look really good with your new jeans, just gently remind yourself that this is your time for a clear mind and try to bring your focus back to your breath. As you breathe out, you can visualise that thought as a cloud that you're pushing away to keep your mind's sky clear and blue.

## HELPFUL HINTS

### Set an alarm

If you find that you get nervous about falling asleep or losing track of time, set an alarm! Setting yourself a goal of doing 10 minutes every day with an alarm is also a really good way to get your body into the practice of meditation – even if for the first few days your brain is awake with loads of thoughts. Gradually, you'll train your mind to recognise 'switch-off time' and it will become calmer more quickly.

### Don't stress about stress!

Don't get frustrated with yourself if you can't switch off your mind. When I'm really stressed I can never get it to stop! One thing I find really useful is to have a pen and paper handy and to write down everything

I'm thinking about – every worry, fear or thought.
Once I have written it down, my mind feels ready
to relax and let go of all the things I wrote down.
Then I can sit with a clear mind.

## Breathe

Everything always comes back to breath – everything
starts here. Make sure you are breathing deep breaths
and letting the tension in your belly fade away.

## Get comfy!

Ideally you want to be sitting or lying in a comfortable
position – I always get cold when I sit still, so I make
sure I have an extra jumper or blanket wrapped around
me before I start. Everyone has a different favourite
position – see what works best for you!

## Find the quiet

You don't want to be trying to meditate in the same
room as someone who is practising how to play a
trumpet or chopping up onions – try and find a quiet
place where you are unlikely to be bothered.

## After-effects

Sometimes after meditating you can be a bit slow
at jumping back into reality, so make sure you take a
second to stand up slowly, check how you feel and take
a deep breath. You may also get hit with inspiration
for how to solve a problem or something you want
to remember, so a pen and paper is always handy.

# 39

# SLEEP

· · · · ·

Apart from food and water, sleep is THE MOST IMPORTANT THING! I mean restful sleep – the kind where you dream about jumping in slow motion across pastel clouds while a brass band plays your favourite song... Going to sleep and waking up at the same time each day is key! It really helps your body clock stay regular. When you don't get enough sleep, everything can seem a bit 'off' the next day and more difficult or annoying. If you can't sleep because you're worrying or thinking about stuff, it can really help to write it down! Keep a pen and paper next to your bed – once you get your worries out of your head and onto paper then your mind is clear to float off to la-la land! You could also try stretching (see page 164), meditating (see page 170) or lavender spray (try a health-food shop.)

176

& works REALLY HARD even while you SLEEP

Please learn to LOVE HER ~ YOUR BODY

— Loren

## 40

# UNHAPPY EATING

· · · · ·

Your 'diet' just means the food and drink you take into your body. Your body needs fuel to work – at least three healthy meals a day, as well as snacks, if you're active and growing. Some people go on 'diets', which usually means they reduce the amount of fuel their bodies take in so they lose weight. But if you are not overweight to begin with, it's dangerous to cut back on your body's fuel. Your energy runs low; your mind can have trouble focusing and your moods change. When I was in secondary school, I never dieted but I had friends who did on and off. I thought it was kinda crazy and pretty boring – the moment someone goes on a diet it seems like all they can think or talk about is food... Anyway, one friend started dieting but something about it was different. She start-ed getting thinner and thinner – everyone was worried about her and tried to get her to eat, but she would say, 'Oh I just ate lunch,' or find some excuse. Eventually she had to leave school and ended up in hospital for a while. She was anorexic and had nearly starved herself to death. It took her a long time to recover but she has managed to get on top of her eating disorder and now she is even a mum herself!

People develop eating disorders for all kinds of reasons, but often as a result of something that happened to them. If they don't feel in control, they may feel that controlling what they eat gives them back power, although this is not logical. Once you have got to a certain point with dieting, your brain starts thinking differently. If you think that you or a friend are starting to obsess about food or aren't eating enough, then there's lots of help out there. Talk to a close adult and do some research – there will be lots of government and health service advice (don't bother with chat rooms – you'll never get the facts there). It's perfectly possible to sort out, and the sooner you do, the better.

# 41

# GIRLS FOR GIRLS

· · · · ·

Pick up any gossip magazine and read the comments made about women. It's as though the only important things for us to worry about are other women's waistlines and whether they're wearing the right clothes. This culture of women putting other women down is an easy habit to fall into in our own lives, but I think it's really sad. It makes people insecure and pits women against one another. It's important to see how destructive this is – competitiveness is for the racetrack; not the street of sisterhood. It's crazy to work against each other – we need to support each other; be a team! The word FEMINISM means different things to different people. For me, it's pretty simple and I couldn't put it better than the great author, Maya Angelou: 'I'm a feminist. I've been a female for a long time now. It'd be stupid not to be on my own side.'

TEAM

MAKE

DREAM

# WORK THE WORK*

*It's not just a catchy phrase
– it's the truth.

## 42

# THAT WAS WEIRD

· · · · ·

As I got older and my body started to change shape, people began looking at me differently. One thing that bugged me a lot was the way men that I didn't know – total strangers – would look at me in this creepy way. For some reason, some men seem to think it's okay not to talk or look at you like you're another person, but to behave as if you're something to be looked at or commented on – as if you're an exhibit in a show or something! It made me feel uncomfortable or like I had done something wrong without knowing it.

One time, when I was really young – maybe eight? – I was in the supermarket and a guy squeezed passed me and also squeezed my bum. URGH, it was so gross! I glared at him – it happened so fast and I was shocked at how he just ignored me and walked off like nothing had happened. I was with my mum (who hadn't seen), but I didn't know what to say, so I said nothing. I was so embarrassed! Later, I began to understand about the importance of speaking up. For nearly 20 years I have played that moment over in my mind, thinking of different versions where I karate chop him in the face! Now I feel a lot more confident to say something or ask for help if something like this happens, but it can be really hard to do. It's difficult because you probably just want the moment to go away as quickly as possible – causing a fuss seems like it's just going to prolong the icky feeling you have or make people wonder what *you* did wrong.

But if you feel safe to act on it there and then, you've got to try and do it! You need to judge the situation – it's so important to be strong and expose this kind of behaviour. And if you don't feel safe to act on it in the moment, please do tell someone you trust as soon as you can after. It'll make you feel better, I promise.

# THE POO STORY

• • • • •

Once, I was at school and the area I was in only had one toilet. I had gone to the toilet during class because I needed to do a massive number two. I always get panicked about #2 because I want it to happen with no one knowing it happened – I always want to disguise it as a #1. So I quickly flush it so it doesn't smell so much,

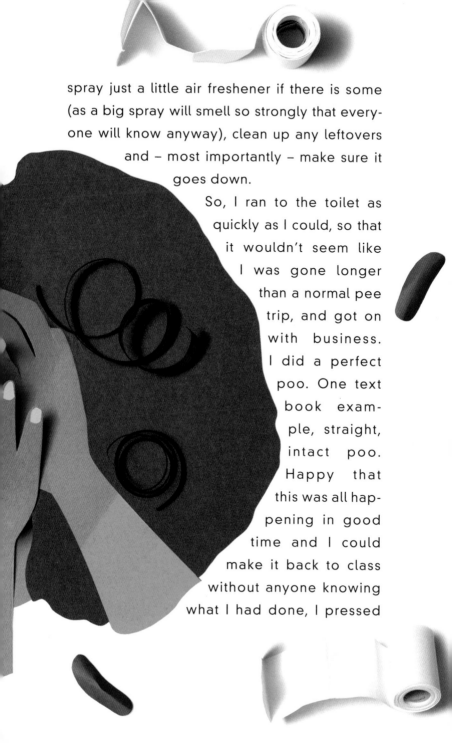

spray just a little air freshener if there is some (as a big spray will smell so strongly that everyone will know anyway), clean up any leftovers and – most importantly – make sure it goes down.

So, I ran to the toilet as quickly as I could, so that it wouldn't seem like I was gone longer than a normal pee trip, and got on with business. I did a perfect poo. One text book example, straight, intact poo. Happy that this was all happening in good time and I could make it back to class without anyone knowing what I had done, I pressed the flush and stood watching, ready to wave goodbye to perfection... Nothing happened. Other than the toilet filling with water a bit. BUT NO SUCK! No flush! No goodbye. My heart started to speed up. Okay, extra water might help it go faster... I pressed flush again and held it down. My poo floated higher and higher as more water flooded the bowl. Horrified, I let go but the water kept coming until, finally, I was left looking at a full bowl of water with a perfect poo slowly bobbing from one side to the other, smiling up at me.

O.M.G.

Remember: one toilet. Whoever went next was going to know that it was me. I couldn't risk flushing one more time. It would overflow for sure. The only option was removal.

I looked around the bathroom at my options. Air freshener? Spray it till it dissolves? Push it down the sink with my bare hands? Toilet paper roll? Scoop it up?

ARGHHHH!!!

Plastic – there was a plastic bin liner in the bin. Okay, this could work. I got the plastic bag.

BUT THEN WHAT? Put it in the bag and what??? I couldn't put it back in the bin. I couldn't take it back to class... The sanitary bin. The sanitary bin with its one-way lid. This was it! Scoop the poo, tie the bag so it didn't smell and put it in the sanitary bin. I had to put my hands in the toilet. Both of them – protected by a thin layer of plastic bag. I scooped and gagged. I tied. I won. The toilet was full of water but that was the next person's problem – there was no evidence of my 'special package'. I washed my hands about 20 times and gave a li'l victory squirt of air freshener... and ran back to class.

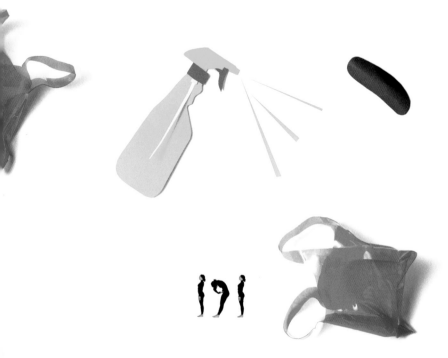

191

# 44

# GIRLS + BOYS

· · · · ·

As kids, my brothers both LOVED wearing dress-es – way more than me. It was never a big deal in my family; just seen as cute. Meanwhile I always thought being a tomboy was cool – it sounded strong and tough, and that's what I wanted to be, so I dressed that way. Not everyone is the same, and there are LOTS of people who don't fit the way they are told they should be. They just want to be themselves and, so long as it's not hurting anyone else, there's no reason why they shouldn't. I say wear the clothes you want, do the things you want, love the people you want.

Almost every film, TV programme and book that you come across as you are growing up will probably have some kind of 'love inter-est' – and it will nearly always be a boy who fancies a girl and/ or a girl who fancies a boy. But that's just not how it is for everyone. Some boys fancy boys. Some girls fancy girls. Some boys feel like they ARE girls, and were born in the wrong bodies. Some girls feel like they are boys in the wrong bodies. It's complicated! Finally, people fall in love with other people, whatever their gender. Fortunately, you live in a time when this is pretty okay. There's far more freedom to be who you are than there was in the past. So, whatever your friends tell you, or your parents want from you – or you want from yourself – you'll figure out who you really are. Don't stress. There's plenty of time! And working it out is half the fun!

# 45

# FASHION vs. STYLE

Okay, so fashion and style are two VERY different things and as soon as you understand the difference between them, you'll feel much more free. Fashion is basically what you see in shop windows or on every second girl at the mall – and it will change regularly. Things that were the IT items last week are suddenly half price and very uncool! Style is more timeless, and is about wearing clothes that suit you and that you love!

Fast fashion can be fun, but it moves on quickly. It's a quick fix and if all you do is fashion, it can be really expensive and annoying because you have to keep buying things to keep up, knowing that in a few weeks or months you wouldn't want to be seen dead in the same outfit. The trick is to mix bits of fashion up with your own style until you find your groove. Style can last a lifetime and change with your mood.

You can find inspiration for your style everywhere – old photographs, magazines, blogs, online, charity shops and markets can all provide inspiration for new looks you might want to try in the safety of your bedroom, before unleashing it on the world. Some people find a look they like and they stick with it forever. Others experiment and try out loads of different looks, hairstyles and accessories. Sometimes it's nice to feel part of a crew with your friends by wearing the same style. This can often be linked to the type of music you listen to or other things you find inspiring at the time. Your style, like your bra size, will probably change a lot over the years. Personally I have been through many phases: Bantu, almost gothic, raver, hip-hop. Embrace trying new things! The great thing about personal style is that when you find things you LOVE to wear, you feel comfortable and confident and this in turn makes you look great! Confidence can often be found in your favourite outfit. Go for it – you only live once!

# THRUSH

· · · · ·

**... AKA 'fire-in-my-pants-I-wanna-sit-in-a-bowl-of-yoghurt!'**

Thrush is a 'yeast infection'. It's caused when tiny yeasty fungi that live in your vagina, called candida, multiply. This leads to a bunch of really irritating symptoms known as THRUSH!

So why do candida start multiplying like crazy? Good question. Stress; tight clothes; changes in your diet; changes in your hormones around the time you get your period; using tampons at the end of your period when your vagina is too dry... all these things can trigger over-production of yeast, leading to thrush.

For most people, the symptoms of thrush are one or any of the following: a white lumpy discharge like cottage cheese and sometimes redness and swelling around the vagina. None of these things will make you feel like the cutest

198

girl in town but just remember it's not a permanent thing and is really easy to cure each time
you get it. Yeast infections affect pretty much all
women at some point. For some it's a one off,
for others it's a re-occurring drama – it is for me.
I had thrush on and off for YEARS and it drove
me CRAZY. I tried everything and I just couldn't
get rid of it. It made me feel gross, hot and
bothered. But now I have a wealth of wonderful
thrush-busting tips to pass on to you!

DON'T worry! Yeast infections
are REALLY common and affect
most people at some point.
However...

DO go to the doctor if you haven't
had it before, just to make sure
you have the right diagnosis.

DON'T wear shiny, synthetic knickers or tights. They won't let your skin breathe, instead creating a little heat trap down there for growing bacteria.

DO wear clean, comfy cotton underpants to let your sensitive skin breathe! You can also get special pure-silk ones, which are great for people with eczema.

DON'T use perfumed soaps, vaginal deodorants (don't use these anyway!) or wipes, as these will just irritate the skin even further.

DO keep your vagina clean. Rinse it loads and wash front to back with lots of clean water once a day.

DON'T think that sitting in a bowl of yoghurt will cure your thrush. But it might help with the symptoms and feel lovely and cool.

DO go to the doctor, who will prescribe you with medication and a cream.

# 47

# FIRE PEE

• • • • •

Once, when I was little, I was running around in a field naked when I managed to get a tiny piece of hay or something stuck right up my pee hole. I didn't realise until I needed the loo and felt a sudden, searing pain. I spent two days refusing to go to the toilet until my mum took me to the doctor, who managed to get it out. Then, when I was older and got an infection up my pee hole (a 'urinary tract infection', or 'UTI'), the burning feeling felt familiar! UTIs are caused by bacteria getting up your pee hole. It's the main reason why we are taught to wipe 'front to back' but other things can bring them on – tight jeans, knickers that aren't made of cotton, and dehydration. I don't mean to put you off all these things, but just so you know! When you have a UTI, you feel like you need to pee the whole time, but when you do it feels like it's burning! Sometimes you also see blood in your urine, so basically the last thing you want to do is pee, but that's one of the most important things to do! You need to drink loads of water to help flush out the infection. If it's bad, you may also need to go to the doctor for antibiotics. ☹

# 48

# STAYING IN CONTROL

. . . . .

This one is so simple: JUST SAY NO. That might be a really boring response, but I am pretty boring when it comes to drug advice – I was never interested. I wanted to be in control of my body. When a lot of my friends started smoking or taking drugs, I would still hang out with them and watch what it did to them and that really put me off! They got really boring and made weird faces. Some people love it – that's their choice and you

get to make your own decisions, too. But drugs can cause real problems with your mental and physical health, so if you want to look after yourself, don't let anyone pressure you into doing anything you don't want to. Easy to say, harder to put into practice, but you need to decide beforehand what you want to do and then stick to it. If someone is going to judge you and make you feel bad for your decisions, then that is their problem and they're not a good friend anyway. My friends just left me alone about it after I said 'no' the first 20 times! They would do their thing and I would make them pancakes. We still had fun – and we ate a lot of great blueberry and banana pancakes together.

# 49

# LAST BUT NOT LEAST

• • • • •

There's so much more I want to tell you! But I have officially run out of room. So here are all the little bits I couldn't get in elsewhere:

Try pants with built-in sanitary pads!
They're amazing. If you look online there
are lots of different brands.

———

Write a letter to your future self – you could write
to your 16-year-old self or 21-year-old self. It's always
fun to write what you think you will be doing when
you are that age – and even weirder to open it up
years later and see how much has changed!

———

Make my energy ball recipe:
Dates, coconut, cacao powder and cranberries.
Mix them all in a blender, then squish into balls and
roll in more coconut – so easy! So tasty! And FULL of
energy. Make them on Sunday and enjoy them all week.

———

Look up Misty Copeland, a solo ballerina
with the American Ballet Theatre. Her story
is amazing and she is so inspiring.

Switch your conditioner from time to time –
don't just stick to one brand. My hair is so much
happier when I swap brands every few months.

———

Look up! Sometimes you find an amazing
building, tree or sight that you have been
walking past all this time...

———

SMILE at yourself in the mirror. I used to do yoga and
the teacher would tell us to do that. I thought it was so
weird and uncomfortable but then I did it and it actually
made me feel happy (probably also because I had
finally finished the yoga class and could go
buy a croissant...)

———

If you use hairbands without the metal bits,
it's much better for your hair – it won't break.

———

Read *I Capture the Castle* by Dodie Smith.
SUCH a great book!

———

Drink more water – it flushes you out!
I always drink two glasses as soon as I wake up.

———

Try half an avocado with lemon or reeaaaally
thinly sliced tomato on toast with cream cheese.

———

Have a go at looking at someone's face and drawing
them, without lifting the pen or looking at what you
are doing. You can make some masterpieces!

———

Write postcards to people – it's great to receive one.

THE
EFFEC
WAY TO
IS TO

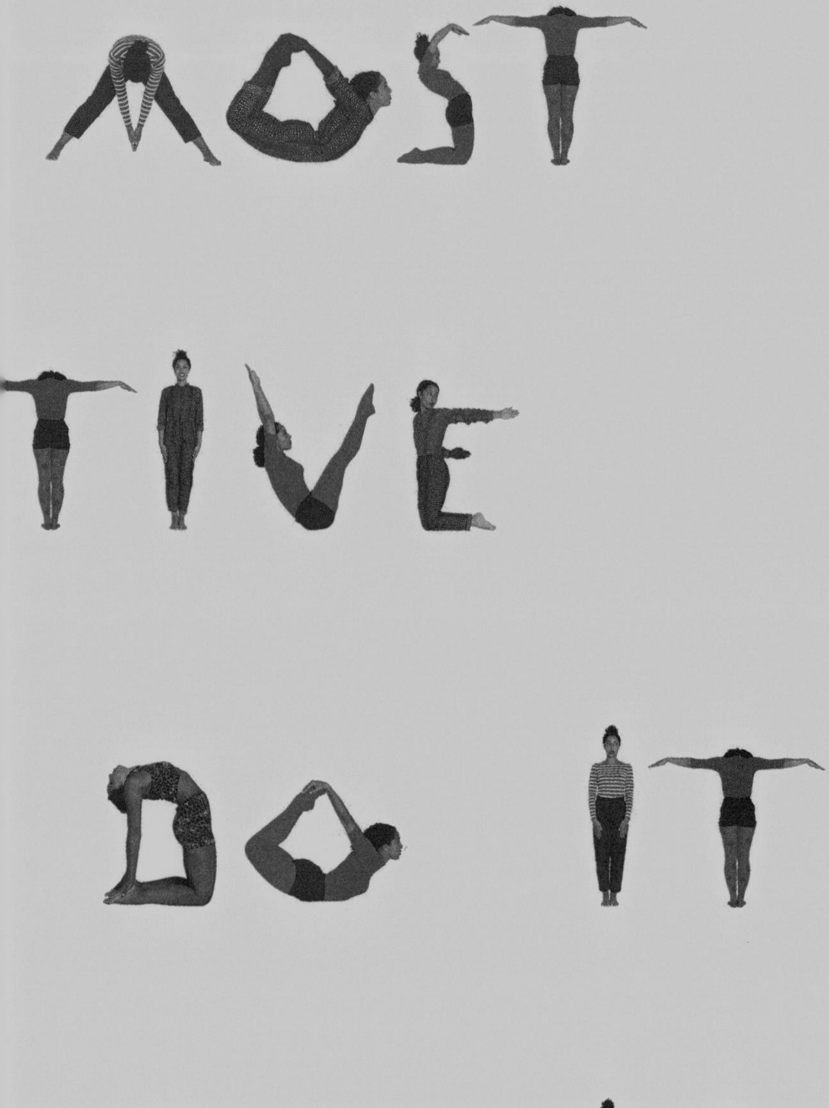

MOST
TIVE
DO IT
DO IT

— Amelia Earhart

# 50

# BUT WHATEVER HAPPENS, KNOW THIS...

· · · · ·

It. Will. All. Be. Okay! I mean it!

Growing up is INTENSE. Everything is unfamiliar and untested and unscripted. Everything is a 'first', once. You don't get to do it twice. You will get some things right the first time but most things, like me, you won't. You will try to avoid leaking periods, moody friends and too much sugar but, like most, you won't. Like every woman in the universe before you, eventually you will have a period crisis; your friends will be too much to handle and then the next day mean everything to you; and every now and then you are going to eat waaay too much sugar. But it's okay! Believe me, we have all done it and survived. Even when the absolutely worst, most embarrassing thing happens and you feel like it's game over – it isn't! Those embarrassing moments will eventually be funny, I promise.

There have been moments for me when I did not believe things would turn out okay but they did anyway. The universe is huuuuge! The world is huge! And we are all just out here trying to make the most of it. Write big lists with BIG DREAMS, even the ones you can't imagine coming true – just write them down! So many of the things I wanted to do but was too embarrassed to even say out loud, I worked towards and eventually made happen. BELIEVE IN YOURSELF. You are your own best friend. PUSH YOURSELF – you can get there!

The one thing I always remember my dad telling me over and over when I was growing up was to leave the world a better place than I found it. At the end of the day, whatever you are doing, that should be in the back of your mind. I never, ever forget it and I check myself all the time and ask myself, 'Is what I am doing useful or helpful?' It doesn't mean you have to drop everything and become an aid worker tomorrow – though kudos to you if that is your dream! – it can be simple things like helping out your friends and family, taking care of yourself so others don't need to, or being a strong and reliable friend.

Time is on your side, sister – the world is yours for the taking! Get out there and make some magic! Everything in this book is something I wish I had known when I was your age. I hope it has given you some good advice and insight for when your body switches it up on you! It's up to you – take this information and run with it, defy it, test it out, throw it to the wind, stomp on it, pin it to the wall, believe it, deny it... do whatever you want with it! Your body is 100% yours and it's AMAZING!

Go for it, little sister.

See you out there somewhere on Planet Earth!

Marawa xx

214

## from Marawa

Stella. Thank you for being an endless source of happy notes and encouraging emails – I thought editing was meant to be like a dentist visit but you made it like a trip to the rollerrink. SINEM! You. Legend. Nobody comes close - I knew as soon as Rachel showed me your work you were the perfect fit for this project. Thank you for sharing your bed with a million balloons and so fabulously communicating the visual elements of this book. Jo Duck - love you forever, you know that - it had to be you.

Majors, Rosa, Maz, Rachel, Clare, Obie THANK YOU for being a part of this. YOU DA BEST. ZEZI - Thank you for the emails and reminders that this book needs to HAPPEN. FINALLY - Maman, who was the human form of this book while I was growing up - an endless source of medical advice, reassurance and support. I don't know how I managed to land the greatest mum of all time but I am so so grateful I did - Thank you for always making me feel like everything is possible. YELD FOR EVER.

## from Sinem

For Tijen and Nessie, who are the most inspirational and selfless women I know; Sena, who is a very strong young girl and beautiful both inside and out; Sema, who always wears a smile and is like a ray of sunshine; Lucia and Willow, for when they turn 10!; Jemma, who is working out how she can replace her pubic hair with paper ones; Lora, who is always sticking up for girls; Madeline, who got me through an all-girls school with her wit; Ella, who might find sections of this book funny; Rachel, our publisher and Stella our skillful editor – without both their amazingness, dedication and grit there would be no *Girl Guide*! – Chris, who lovingly assisted with making some of the paper props and Jo, who bought my concepts and rough drawings to life with the photographs starring Marawa. And of course MARAWA who is such a star, sooo energising and an absolute joy to work with!

First published in the UK in 2017 by
Frances Lincoln Children's Books,
an imprint of The Quarto Group
The Old Brewery
6 Blundell Street
London N7 9BH
QuartoKnows.com

Visit our blogs at QuartoKids.com

Important: there are age restrictions for most blogging and social
media sites and in many countries parental consent is also required.
Always ask permission from your parents.

Website information is correct at time of going to press. However, the
publishers cannot accept liability for any information or links found
on any Internet sites, including third-party websites.

Art Direction, Graphic Design, Illustrations,
Prop making and Set Designs by Sinem Erkas
All photography starring Marawa / the Majorettes by Jo Duck
Stretch mark photos © Getty Images and Alamy

Edited by Stella Gurney
Published by Rachel Williams

Printed in China
9 8 7 6 5 4 3 2 1

# IN THE MAKING OF THIS BOOK

Marawa and Sinem were introduced over breakfast in London

It took Marawa 2.26 minutes to solve the maze on p.120

It took 5 attempts to make the Jelly on p.142

Marawa and the majorettes all braved tights with no knickers to get the amazing bum mountain shot! Sinem hand-dyed the tights to make a nice sunset (p.150)

Marawa had real spots on her face being covered up by 72 googly eyes (including one that Sinem put half-way in her nose – yuck!) (p.22)

Dress rehearsals were done in Marawa's bathroom and at the Hoopermarket

All of the paper bras were made life-size

Sinem and Marawa discussed the book layout, including the vagina chapters, in various London restaurants

Marawa broke a full-length mirror at The Russian Club in London, where we did the photo shoots

Marawa shaved off ALL HER HAIR half way through the project and we decided to re-shoot the introduction as a recreation of her 10 year-old photo

Sinem (whilst working out how to achieve the meditation shot) fell over and bruised her arm after trying to levitate! Luckily, Marawa is actually circus trained! (p.147)

Sinem set Marawa homework to practise the letter poses every day for two weeks, which became Marawa's morning yoga routine

To create all of the paper props and sets, Sinem got through approx. 30 metres of paper, 2 rolls of gaffer tape, 2 rolls of masking tape, 2 rolls of double sided tape, 3 packs of sticky pads, some glue, 4 metres of card and 240 cups of coffee

Purple tinsel made the pubic hair (p.65)

Marawa made 156 letters and 30 numbers with her body in one day

Sinem left her giant eyeballs (which took 5 hours to make) in a box with Marawa, which BLEW OPEN as Marawa's taxi arrived. She had to chase them all the way down the road! She kept this a secret until after the shoot (p.11)

but they were not comfy to wear

Sinem had to give up her bed for a night to create the image on p.35, as the balloons took over her whole bedroom

White PVC was used to make the yoghurt on p.199

Email meetings were held everywhere as Marawa travelled between the UK, US, France, Mexico, Australia, Spain, Cuba and Hawaii

Sponges & washing -up liquid were used to create the pancakes and syrup on p.207

MARAWA BROKE 4 WORLD RECORDS!!

In real life, the paper vagina illustrations are A4 in size. Paper pubic hairs found themselves everywhere for days after photographing them (p.52)

Whilst arranging the paper spots, Sinem sneezed and they blew into position a lot better than how she originally had them (p.22)

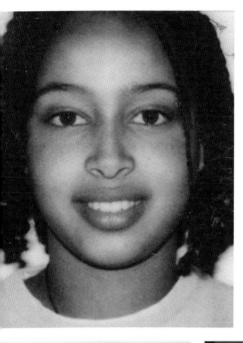